C000068299

Sixteenth-Century St. Augustine

ALBERT MANUCY

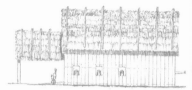

University Press of Florida

GAINESVILLE TALLAHASSEE TAMPA BOCA RATON

PENSACOLA ORLANDO MIAMI JACKSONVILLE

SIXTEENTH-CENTURY

st. augustine

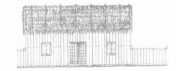

The People and Their Homes

Copyright 1997 by the Board of Regents of the State of Florida
Printed in the United States of America on acid-free paper
All rights reserved

02 01 00 99 98 97 6 5 4 3 2 1

LIBRARY OF CONGRESS CATALOGING-IN-PUBLICATION DATA
Manucy, Albert C.
Sixteenth-century St. Augustine: the people and their homes / Albert Manucy.
p. cm.
Includes bibliographical references and index.
ISBN 0-8130-1484-0 (alk. paper).
1. Saint Augustine (Fla.)—Antiquities. 2. Dwellings—Florida—Saint Augustine—
History—16th century. 3. Architecture, Domestic—Florida—Saint Augustine—
History—16th century. 4. Spaniards—Florida—Saint Augustine—Antiquities.
I. Title.
F319.S2M34   1997
975.9'18—DC20   96-31964

The University Press of Florida is the scholarly publishing agency for the State
University System of Florida, comprised of Florida A & M University, Florida
Atlantic University, Florida International University, Florida State University,
University of Central Florida, University of Florida, University of North Florida,
University of South Florida, and University of West Florida.

University Press of Florida
15 Northwest 15th Street
Gainesville, FL 32611

This book is dedicated to Lawrence Lewis Jr., who inspired and fostered the research into the early days of his beloved city. I was not alone in this quest for knowledge. Lawrence and his executive, Bill Rolleston, brought historians Eugene Lyon and Paul Hoffman, anthropologist Francisco Aguilera, and archaeologist Kathleen Deagan into the project. A number of their contributions are listed in the bibliography at the end of this book. Not only were their sources helpful, but it was a pleasure working with the authors.

Contents

Figures, Maps, and Table

MAPS

TABLE

Preface

MY INTEREST IN historic houses began in my childhood in St. Augustine. Grandmother Evalina was a widow with two houses, and she liked to move from one to the other. Her smaller house at 41 Abbott Street was my birthplace, but I did most of my growing at 18 St. George Street, just one block from the city gate and the fort (Castillo de San Marcos) green, and three blocks from the bay.

In those days some of the old houses were being torn down and replaced by new structures, and little kids (I was one) liked to investigate the rubble. I remember an old frame house on Cuna Street: the interior walls were wooden laths covered with lime plaster, and hair was mixed into the plaster to strengthen it. Castillo de San Marcos seemed a mysterious background in those childhood days, but the colorful parades, pageants, and reenactments performed annually at the old fort told its story time and time again.

When I became a student at the University of Florida, my interest in historical architecture burgeoned. I was in the College of Education when I learned that the School of Architecture was offering art courses. I had been art editor for my high school annual and was sure I needed more instruction. I got it; I have more college credits in fine arts than in education. I also learned a lot about architectural history, taught by the school's director, Rudolph Weaver.

I graduated from college in the Depression years. Jobs were scarce, so I went back to work on my master of arts. My thesis was "A Comparison of Certain Plans of Beaumont and Fletcher with Their Sources in Cervantes' Novelas Ejemplares." I was beginning to feel like a linguist: Latin and Spanish in high school, more Spanish and English in college, and Anglo-Saxon, Spanish, and English in graduate school. Later I would add some German and Italian—but not much!

It was 1934 when I met Herbert Kahler. He was a National Park Service (NPS) historian who came to St. Augustine to bring the Castillo and Fort Matanzas into the National Park system. I worked briefly for Herb as a researcher, then he sent me to Key West to head a Works Progress Administration project to research the history of Fort Jefferson National Monument. Jefferson is a big brick fort of the 1840s in the Dry Tortugas Islands west of Key West, but its documents were filed in the Key West Army Post. When the money for the project ran out, Dr. Carita Corse, state director of the Federal Writers' Project, sent me back to St. Augustine to put together a guidebook, *Seeing St. Augustine*. That was accomplished in 1937.

Meanwhile, St. Augustine's mayor, Walter Fraser, got together with Judge David Dunham, president of the St. Augustine Historical Society; Dr. John Merriam, president of the Carnegie Institution of Washington; and Verne "Chat" Chatelain, formerly chief historian of the National Park Service, and the St. Augustine Historical Program was born. Carita Corse, with the guidebook finished, handed me and the typists over to Chatelain and the Historical Program. At that time the John B. Stetson photographic collections of Spanish records were in Tacoma Park, Maryland, in the care of state archivist James Robertson. Chat took my wife Clara and me to search those documents and the Library of Congress for St. Augustine information. The search was successful, and Chat published his *Defenses of Spanish Florida, 1565 to 1763* in 1941.

When I was in Key West, Herb Kahler had advised me to take the Civil Service exam for historian, and I did. In November 1938 I began my thirty-three-year career with the National Park Service as historian at Castillo de San Marcos. My job was multifaceted: I was to research the history of the Castillo and Fort Matanzas and train the tour guides; write a folder handout; compile a source book of historical documents; write an illustrated history of the forts; plan and construct museum exhibits; plan reconstructions of drawbridges, doors, bunks, and gun carriages; and research and plan reconstruction of the palisaded earthwork that connects the Castillo and the city gate.

To do all that, one needed Spanish records. Working in the Library of Congress, I had used the Woodbury Lowery Collection (ten volumes of transcripts from Spanish and French archives) as well as the Stetson Collection, at that time in Maryland. Then when I became Castillo historian I had the good fortune to learn from Lucy L. Wenhold about the photostats of Spanish records in the North Carolina Archives and microfilmed them for the Castillo.

Research on the cannon carriages led to my writing a book on artillery (1949), but I did not have a title for it. When Superintendent Ray Vinten read the manuscript he said, "Artillery through the Ages," which solved the problem.

In those days the NPS did not have many historians, so I had some extra assignments: *Historic Site Survey of the Panama Canal Zone* (1957); Interpretive Survey Team for Independence National Historical Park (1959); *The Fort at Frederica* (1960); NPS research and museum mission in Spain, Holland, and England (1962). With me on the European search was Julio Marrero, historian at San Juan National Historic Site in Puerto Rico. While we were in Madrid, Julio got a phone call: He was no longer historian; he had been promoted to superintendent! Fortunately our work in Spain was almost done.

I could not have had a better partner than Julio. He knew a lot of people in Spain, and now I did too. Example: I met Rafael Fernández-Huidobro, professor of architecture at Madrid University. I had just finished writing *The Houses of St. Augustine, 1565– 1821*, and I told the professor that I wanted to study Spain's folk architecture to see what influence it may have had upon housing in St. Augustine. It was the beginning of a productive twenty-year friendship.

With the help of Earle Newton, director of the St. Augustine Historical and Preservation Commission, in 1962 I received a Fulbright grant to spend a year in Spain studying folk architecture. With leave of absence from the NPS, plus enthusiastic support from my wife Clara and our teenagers Evalina and James, we went to Spain and traveled ten thousand miles in our little Volkswagen. We were a good team: I was front-seat passenger with notebook and camera ready; Clara was chauffeur; Evalina read the maps; and James handled the baggage. Many a time I thanked Miss Leone Rood, my high school Spanish teacher. In Spain my thanks were audibly given to Ramón Bela, director of the Fulbright Commission in Madrid; Juan de Contreras, Marqués de Lozoya, a professor at Madrid University; Juan Manuel

Zapatero, director of the Military History Archive; Col. José Hernández Ballesteros of the Artillery Museum; Julio Guillen Tato, director of the Naval Museum; Arturo Gran Fernández, secretary of Amigos de los Castillos; and José de la Peña y Cámara, director of the Archivo General de Indias, the great repository for the history of the colonial Americas.

And there were many others—the people who lived in the houses I came to see. They were pleased at my interest and gladly showed me their homes (I'm sure it helped to have my family along). I learned a lot, and I took a lot of it home: six field notebooks (448 pages of notes and sketches), seven notebooks with detailed drawings, five notebooks (280 pages) of library notes, and 460 photographs plus 320 in color.

In 1966 I was promoted to curator and moved to the NPS Southeast Regional Office in Richmond. There my dear wife Clara died in 1970. I retired from the National Park Service in 1971 with the idea of spending another year in Spain, but instead I married Elsie. She had resigned from the NPS to work for the U.S. Army in Germany, so we lived in Germany. But Elsie liked to travel, so travel we did—France, England, the Holy Land, the Far East—and I still had time to write (with NPS historian Ricardo Torres-Reyes) *Puerto Rico and the Forts of Old San Juan.*

When Elsie's contract in Germany ran out, we spent a year and ten thousand more miles in Spain recording architecture, people, scenery, and timberframe. This time my friend Huidobro introduced me to Carlos Flores, a former student who was publishing *Arquitectura Popular España*, five huge volumes with hundreds of photographs, many in color, of folk architecture in all parts of Spain. When I met Carlos in 1973, only his first volume was printed; volume 5 came in 1977. All five are now on my library shelf for ready reference. I'm glad they are there, but I'm also glad that I didn't have them in 1962 when Clara, the kids, and I enjoyed traveling ten thousand miles on our own, finding old homes and talking with the people.

Back in St. Augustine, Lawrence Lewis talked with our mutual friend Bill Rolleston about a project that would reconstruct early St. Augustine. Bill knew of my interest in historic housing, and he came to Spain while Elsie and I were there. Because the early builders in Florida did not have stone to work with, Bill and I decided to search for ancient wooden construction in Spain. The result was my 113-page *Traditional Timberframe in Spain*, with sixty-seven photographs and drawings.

Bill asked me to join Lawrence's St. Augustine Restoration Foundation, which I did, moving back to St. Augustine in January 1975. Already on the staff were two historians, Paul Hoffman and Eugene Lyon, both of them Ph.D.'s with experience in Spanish archives. They provided detailed information about the San Agustín people—soldiers, settlers, missionaries, Indians—and about many other things, including fortifications, housing, weapons, and food supplies. Archaeologist Kathleen Deagan wrote a "Research and Exhibit Plan for a 1580 Timucua Village near St. Augustine"; Curator Frank Aguilera reported on *Acquisition of Specified Items of Material Culture and Technology for Saint Augustine 1580*. I worked up *Plot Plans: The 1580 Town*. These titles were but a few of the reports that detailed information recovered from archives and archaeology.

Lawrence decided that the logical and best way to reconstruct St. Augustine 1580 was on film, and this was done. *Dream of Empire* is the film's title, and it takes the audience back to the sixteenth century by showing the achievements and tragedies, the failures and successes of the people from this period. For present-day St. Augustinians and visitors it is an interesting human history lesson.

But what about the source material, the hundreds of Spanish archival documents microfilmed for study by the Foundation historians? They are deposited in Flagler College's Center for Historic Research, along with the multitude of research reports prepared by the Foundation staff. Dr. Eugene Lyon directs the Center.

In writing this book, I used the documents and staff reports now in the Center plus my decades of research on Spain's folk architecture, which is linked to the colonial constructions of St. Augustine. I am indebted to many people for making this work possible, although I can name but a few: I'm thankful for Miss Rood's teaching me Spanish; for Director Weaver's course in architectural history; for my NPS colleagues; for the opportunities Lawrence Lewis made possible; for the encouragement of Jean Parker Waterbury and Page Edwards of the St. Augustine Historical Society; for editor Walda Metcalf of the University Press of Florida. And I am especially grateful for the tolerance and cooperation of my family through the years.

Archaeological Background

AMATEUR ARCHAEOLOGISTS first sparked professionals' curiosity about the early settlement in St. Augustine when a hundred years ago they began digging into the shell middens along the waterways.[1] But the first professional work at St. Augustine was instigated in the 1930s by Mayor Walter B. Fraser, owner of the Fountain of Youth Park, after he found historic burials in his property. In 1934 archaeologist Ray Dickson uncovered more than a hundred burials at the site, and in 1935 state archaeologist Vernon Lamme located the nearby Timucua Indian village.

The next year Fraser interested John Merriam, president of the Carnegie Institution of Washington, in the potential for St. Augustine's historical preservation and restoration. Other national and local organizations, with individuals, joined to establish the St. Augustine Historical Preservation and Restoration Association. Funded by the Carnegie Institution, along with state and local governments and organizations, the St. Augustine Historical Program produced research and development plans, concentrating, up to World War II, on the military aspects of Spanish St. Augustine.

In the 1950s the Fountain of Youth site regained the active interest of archaeologists, resulting in excavations and studies. Over succeeding decades their work has added to the knowledge of what went on in that area through past centuries.

A wider study of archaeological possibilities appeared in November 1976: "A Sub-Surface Survey of the St. Augustine City Environs" by Kathleen Deagan, John Bostwick, and Dale Benton. Sinking auger holes at various locations, the surveyors aimed to discover "the physical extent of 16th, 17th and 18th century St. Augustine" through "the recovery and distribution patterning of sub-surface material within the survey area." In terms of artifacts recovered by the auger survey, sixteenth-century occupation was concentrated in a core bordered by Artillery Lane, Marine Street, Bridge Street, and St. George Street. In the two blocks south of Bridge Street there were fewer artifacts, but there were more in the northwest and southeast corners of the central core.[2]

In 1978 Deagan worked several town sites where the auger had exposed sixteenth-century evidence. She found postmolds, clay daub and other structural evidence, iron objects, trash pits, a barrel well, ceramics (including olive jars and glass vials), animal remains (deer, pig, chicken, oysters, gopher turtle, fish), and evidence of other foods (peach pits, squash, gourds).[3]

The auger was also used at the Fountain of Youth Park, and in 1985 Edward Chaney's excavations revealed that Indian occupation of the site dated back to the Orange period (ca. 1500 B.C. to ca. A.D. 200), which was named after the Orange Site in Volusia County where distinctive early pottery was first found. Two shell middens in the eastern area of the site date from this early period. Two later middens are north and south of the village where the old Orange period pottery was supplanted by a chalky variety that archaeologists call St. Johns (figure 1.1). Add to these findings the discovery of European (that is, Spanish) artifacts, including 65-caliber lead balls that were definitely not Indian, and what results is positive evidence of a Spanish settlement.[4]

Gardner Gordon worked the Fountain of Youth site in 1992 and completed a detailed fifty-seven-page report on his findings in areas with a mix of pre-Columbian Indian and Spanish artifacts. In the introduction to Gordon's report, Deagan (principal investigator for the project) summarized progress in the recent years and concluded that the area known as Seloy Village was definitely the encampment for the Spanish newcomers in 1565.

Continuing archaeological study of the area supports and broadens that conclusion. Knowledge of sixteenth-century St. Augustine is continually expanded by the rich discoveries that give evidence of the San Agustín long ago familiar to soldiers, settlers, and the Timucua.

෴ ෴ ෴

In addition to relying upon clues recovered by archaeologists and upon cartographic evidence of board-and-thatch construction, I have drawn upon the photographs and sketch details of traditional folk architecture made during my two years of fieldwork in Spain.

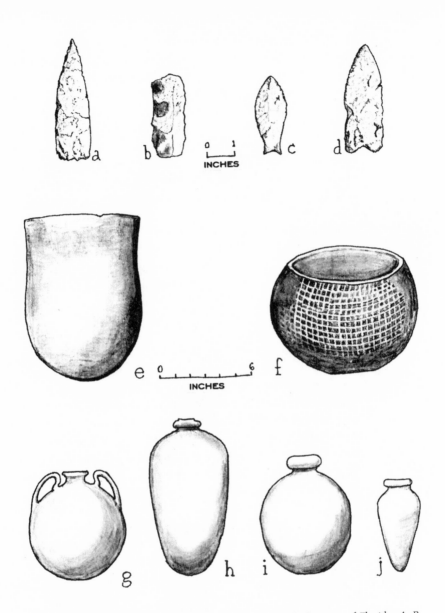

FIGURE 1.1. Artifacts. *A–D:* stone tools made by the early hunters of Florida. *A, B:* knife blades; *C, D:* spear points. *E–F:* St. Johns pottery. *E:* St. Johns Plain (about 1000 B.C.); *F:* St. Johns Check Stamped. *G–J:* Spanish olive jar shapes. *G:* Early Period (ca. A.D. 1500–80); *H–J:* Middle Period (ca. A.D.1580–1780). Spanish-made olive jars were strong containers that were used to convey olive oil and other liquids to the Americas, where the jars became kitchen fixtures. Courtesy of the St. Augustine Historical Society.

Spanish architectural traditions were adapted in Florida by the settlers; they also adapted and used Timucuan building methods.

Some of the Indians built for the new settlers, such as Capt. Juan de Junco. A hut of palm fronds was built for Junco wth the aid of two soldiers; it cost him nothing. (The hut and corral were built for two shepherds who cared for the king's goats.) In 1588 the Indian chief at Nombre de Dios (Name of God) was paid 130 reales for furnishing 1,300 palm fronds to make a house in the fort. There was no mention of who built the house, but most likely it was soldiers—perhaps the very ones who helped build the shepherds' hut.

One thing is certain: The Spaniards did not want the Indians' round huts. In Spain there were rectangular lots contained within rectangular blocks, usually with rectangular houses within the lots; and the same rectangular regularity prevailed in Spain's colonies.

છ છ છ

Sixteenth-Century St. Augustine: The People and Their Homes describes the first years in the settlement of St. Augustine, especially between 1565 and 1600, and is meant to be a companion to *The Houses of St. Augustine.* I have focused in this volume on how the first Spanish colonists lived and what their early buildings and backyards were like. As for architecture, detailed information is sparse indeed. My reconstructions are necessarily conjectural. Contemporary building practices were matters of common knowledge and of little interest to letter writers, and they seldom were mentioned unless a building was of unusual importance, such as the big wooden fort extant in St. Augustine in 1580.

As ensuing chapters disclose, there is much more to the relationship between the Florida Spaniards and the Florida Indians. Chapter 2, "How It Began," gives a historical overview of how and why the Spanish, and especially Pedro Menéndez, came to settle Florida.

Chapter 3, "Early Days," recounts the early days of Spanish presence in the new colony and Menéndez's plans for his "La Florida." This chapter also introduces the Timucua as well as the French cartographer and artist Jacques Le Moyne. I have based my house-type drawings mainly, but not solely, upon Le Moyne's overview of a Timucua village.

In Chapter 4, "An Unsettled Settlement," I trace the history of the nine wooden forts of San Agustín that preceded Castillo de San Marcos, the stone fort. Chapter 5, "Two Accounts, Two Maps," reveals the hard life of settlers in a hostile environment unfit for farming or raising stock and beset by poverty and hunger.

Chapter 6, "Materials That Built the Town," explores native building materials that were used to construct various types of shelter, including dwellings and fortifications.

Chapter 7, "People, Plans, Shelters," looks at plot plans and backyards that were uncovered in archaeological excavations in St. Augustine. Archaeology and the study of the social structure of sixteenth-century Spain provide the context for analysis and interpretation of the new settlement. Three social classes are introduced: upper, middle, and lower.

Chapter 8, "Humble Homes," introduces the documented owners of the lower-class homes, such as Francisco González, drummer and town crier. Chapter 9, "Middle-Class Homes," explores middle-class housing through the dwellings of chief carpenter Martín de Yztueta and others. Accompanying Menéndez to Florida, Yztueta most likely is the man responsible for bringing board walls to St. Augustine. Finally, Chapter 10, "Upper-Class Homes," depicts the houses and plot plans of the upper class, including property owned by Doña Maria de Pomar that eventually was bought by a colonial governor.

❧ ❧ ❧

Although none of the first colonial houses of St. Augustine remain, it is clear from the later survivors that they are related to the folk architecture of northern Spain, the home of Pedro Menéndez, the town's founder. Today in Oviedo and Santander Provinces one can see masonry houses, often with overhead balconies, fronting the streets. House lots are fenced to serve as corrals and stables. And in the town of Treceño there are houses with roomy ground-floor loggias, open to the yard through an arcade of two or three arches. These same styles can be seen in St. Augustine, and they have been there a long time.

How It Began

MAYBE IT BEGAN when Felipe of Aragón married Isabella of Castile in A.D. 1469. That marriage of the Catholic kings led to the unification of Spain, except for the Moorish kingdom of Granada. In 1492 the Catholic kings brought even Granada into their kingdom. Christopher Columbus had been seeking help from Isabella to finance his search for a new route to the Orient, but she was too busy to bother. Now, with Granada in hand, she became his sponsor, and Columbus found the "new" world of the Americas.

Pope Alexander VI gave the monopoly of the Americas to Spain, but Portugal complained that the pope's boundary line did not give Portugal's ships the sea room needed to sail around Africa. So, by the Treaty of Tordesillas (1494), Spain and Portugal moved the pope's line a bit westward, which is the reason Brazilians speak Portuguese today.

The Spaniards had learned fighting skills during centuries of intermittent warfare with the Moors. Now they brought those skills, along with their culture and Catholicism, to the Americas. And as the sixteenth century unfolded, all of Europe saw this new world as abounding in gold and silver as well as opportunities for settlement.[1]

Pedro Menéndez de Avilés was born to adventure. He went to sea early, fighting French corsairs along the Spanish coasts in the 1540s. He soon had his own vessel, with permission from the Crown to hunt corsairs all twelve months of the year. In 1550–51 he made his first voyage to the Indies.

By the time he was thirty-five, as captain general of the Indies fleet in 1555–56, Menéndez convoyed ships that brought cargoes of treasure from its colonies to Spain. It was on his return from that voyage that the Casa de Contratación, the governing board for the American trade, accused Menéndez of smuggling. After he was cleared of the charges, Philip II named him captain general for the 1560 Indies convoy and then again in 1561 and 1562. More legal troubles with the Casa arose when Menéndez reached Spain in 1563, but by early 1565 all charges against him had been dismissed.

This was at a time when Philip faced decisions on a Spanish move to plant colonies in Florida. For his king Menéndez produced a memorial on the area's coasts, on the probable French threat to Spain's interest in the peninsula, and on the means to deal with such a threat. Determined that Spain alone should settle Florida, Philip and the Council of the Indies signed an agreement with Menéndez. He should lead the enterprise as *adelantado* (governor) and captain general (figure 2.1).

Historian Eugene Lyon, for his book *The Enterprise of Florida*, read uncounted documents in Spain's archives and extracted therefrom long-forgotten details of Pedro Menéndez's planning, which included the articles needed for the Florida enterprise: men, women, and children; food and wines; firearms, cannons, munitions, and projectiles; marine supplies; tools; iron and steel; fishnets; cloth for trade; footwear; eight church bells; and altar furnishings.[2]

As preparations for the expedition got under way, Philip learned of the 1564 establishment in Florida of Fort Caroline, a French Huguenot settlement at the mouth of what is today known as the

FIGURE 2.1. Pedro Menéndez de Avilés. Courtesy of the St. Augustine Historical Society.

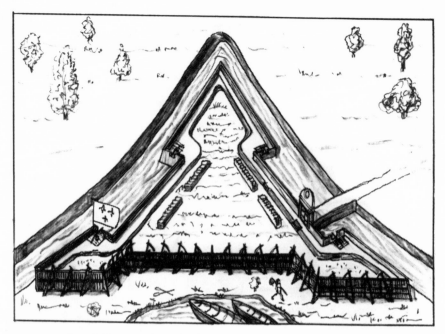

FIGURE 2.2. French Fort Caroline. The fort was built in the summer of 1564 on the south shore of the St. Johns River. The board wall at the riverfront was anchored by timber props. A moat was dug along the other fronts, and its soil was compacted into a nine-foot-high earthwork. Courtesy of the St. Augustine Historical Society.

St. Johns River. Added impetus to Menéndez's assignment came within weeks in a report to Philip that French reinforcements under Jean Ribault were about to sail from Dieppe for Fort Caroline (figure 2.2).

Ribault left France on May 22, 1565, with specific orders from Adm. Gaspard de Coligny: "Do not let Menéndez encroach upon you." Menéndez left Cadiz on June 29, 1565, with equally specific orders from Philip II: "You will explore and colonize Florida; and if there be settlers or corsairs of other nations not subject to us, drive them out."[3]

Early Days

"If there be settlers or corsairs of other nations . . . drive them out." That was King Philip's order as Pedro Menéndez agreed to colonize Florida. On Saint Augustine's Day, August 28, 1565, Menéndez with five of his vessels reached the Florida coast and sailed northward looking for the French colony that inspired Philip's order. He came to "a good harbor with a good beach," which he named San Agustín. The next day he sailed on, and at the mouth of the St. Johns River he found four French galleons anchored.

Speaking French to the crew of the flagship *Trinity*, Menéndez told them he was there "to hang the heretics" and would board their ships at dawn. They invited him to start the fight at once, but when they saw him begin to accept the challenge, they cut their cables and sailed away. With storm-damaged, heavily laden vessels, Menéndez could not catch them, so he sailed back to San Agustín harbor.[1]

He needed a foothold before he could carry out King Philip's orders. On September 6 he sent two infantry companies ashore with captains Andrés Sóyez Patiño and Juan de San Vicente. There was an Indian village on the west side of the harbor, and the Spaniards were well received by the cacique of Seloy. He offered the Spaniards the communal Great House for a shelter (figure 3.1).[2]

Even before the French threat was eliminated, San Agustín began to take shape. On September 6 two captains set their men to making the Great House into a defense. They dug a moat around it and used the soil from the moat to make a breastwork of earth and fascines (bundles of sticks bound together). They dug this earthwork "with only their fingernails," says the record, because tools were aboard a ship that had not yet arrived.[3]

On September 7 the smaller vessels came over the bar and landed three hundred more people, including women and children. Twenty bronze cannons also were put ashore. September 8 was

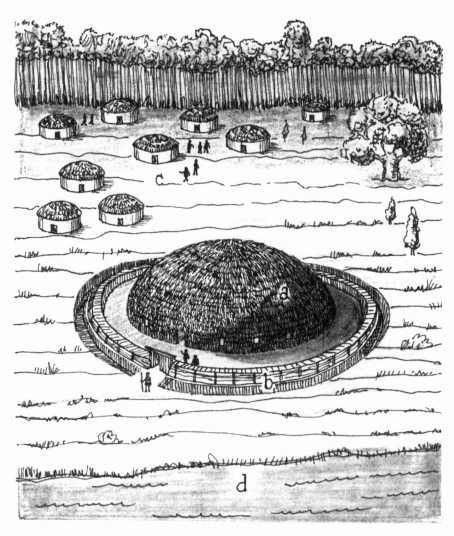

FIGURE 3.1. Seloy's Great House. *A:* residence and meeting place of the Timucuan chief Seloy; it was roomy enough to gather all the village people, and Seloy let the Spanish occupy it. *B:* moat and earthwork built by soldiers around the big dome for defense. *C:* Timucuan village nearby. *D:* the bay. Courtesy of the St. Augustine Historical Society.

Saturday. Two French ships appeared offshore, then sailed back north to report the Spanish doings to their leader. Meanwhile, the last hundred people debarked, and in mid-afternoon Menéndez came ashore. The people—and the Indians—were waiting, and when Don Pedro set foot on Florida soil, Father López, the chaplain, came forward with the cross and offered mass.

Pedro Menéndez proclaimed possession of the land in the name of the Crown of Spain. The landing site was christened "Nombre de Dios" (Name of God), and it still bears that title. After the ceremony Menéndez inspected the defense his captains had made; he was pleased.

Three days later six French vessels loaded with soldiers were sighted off the harbor, but a sudden storm beached them far to the south. Menéndez and his men marched north through the storm and took the French Fort Caroline. Later they captured most of the castaways and put them to the sword. He reported the successes to King Philip, who responded, "We hold ourselves well served."[4]

☙ ☙ ☙

Menéndez's plans for his La Florida—its conquest, pacification, and evangelization—included the establishment of a military and settler presence at port cities and economic development. These goals required good relations with the Indians. Those whom he had first encountered, the people of the cacique Seloy, were Timucuas, long occupants of the area between the St. Mary's River and Matanzas Inlet, west to the St. Johns and beyond to the Suwannee River (map 3.1).[5]

The French artist Jacques Le Moyne, one of the Fort Caroline settlers, was in contact with the Timucua for more than a year until he escaped Menéndez's forces in September 1565. His drawings depict the people with whom the Spaniards dealt in their first days in San Agustín.[6] The Timucuas were powerfully built, strong swimmers, and bold warriors. Males wore deerskin breechclouts or nothing. Females made short skirts from Spanish moss (*Tillandsia usneoides*), and that was all they wore except for shells, feathers, fish teeth, pearls, metal disks, fish-bladder earrings, and such. They let their hair flow down their backs, unless they were widows (figure 3.2). When a woman lost her man, she cut her hair short and did not marry again until it was shoulder

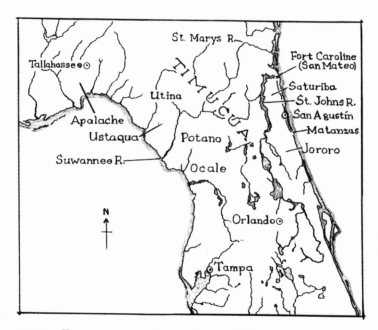

MAP 3.1. Timucua territory. The map locates six Timucua areas, each with the name of a sixteenth-century chief. A seventh area, Apalache in western Florida, was not Timucuan but rather part of the Apalachee culture. In later years it became a Spanish mission area and food source for San Agustín. The Spanish settlements were San Agustín and San Mateo (the Spanish name for Fort Caroline after its capture). Matanzas Inlet, where the shipwrecked Frenchmen surrendered, became the site of a Spanish watchtower. For present-day orientation, I have included Tallahassee, Tampa, and Orlando. Jacksonville, not shown, is just across the St. Johns from San Mateo. Courtesy of the St. Augustine Historical Society.

length. Each man tied his long hair into a topknot, then put a circlet around the head that fluffed the hair into a sort of hat brim, a receptacle for feathers or other decorations.

Both Indians and Spaniards wanted to trade. The soldiers and colonists came prepared with cheap items to exchange for bullion, pearls, or other items that would have much value in Europe. From the Indian viewpoint, trading useless gold or silver, which they had salvaged from Spanish wrecks, for an iron ax head was a real bargain. The Indians were also interested in other available items: weapons, building and farming tools, nails, bells, glass beads, rum, cloth, and blankets.[7] And the natives had many things the Spanish (and others) wanted: sassafras (a medicine), amber, deer and buffalo skins, nut oil, bear grease, tobacco, canoes, pottery—and food. Amy Bushnell gives details:

The swamps and savannahs provided edible roots, wild fruit, and game; lakes and rivers were full of fish; oysters grew huge in the arms of the sea. Indians paddling canoes or carrying baskets brought their produce to the market on the plaza; twists of tobacco, pelts, painted wooden trays, packages of dried cassina tea leaves, rope and fishnets, earthenware and baskets, dried turkey meat, lard and salt pork, saddles and shoe leather, charcoal and fresh fish and game; but especially they brought maize. . . . When maize crops were hurt, St. Augustine was hungry.[8]

Eugene Lyon has pointed out that "cultural brokers" between the Timucuas and the Spaniards had an essential role in Menéndez's program. Who were they? Number one was Pedro Menéndez; he got along well with most Indian leaders. So did some later governors, but others did not. In the early days, when almost no Spaniards could speak the Indian tongues, there were a few Spanish castaways or Frenchmen living with the Indians. Some of them were recruited as interpreters. In later times soldiers married Indian women, learned the Timucua language and customs, and became interpreters. Some of these soldier-interpreters became soldier-enforcers for collecting food or tribute from the

FIGURE 3.2. Timucua males and females toiling in the fields. Jacques Le Moyne made forty or more drawings depicting the lifestyle of the Timucuas. Courtesy of the St. Augustine Historical Society.

Indians. Some of their wives also learned Spanish and became useful negotiators. These men and women, Spanish and Timucua, worked hard to establish and maintain good relationships.

There also were private traders among the settlers and soldiers. Their work was monitored—and sometimes confiscated—by their leaders.[9]

❧ ❧ ❧

Remnants of the Seloy familiar to the Spaniards exist today in the archaeological discoveries at St. Augustine's Fountain of Youth Park, positive evidence of aboriginal structures that were part of sixteenth-century Seloy. Excavations in 1951 uncovered remains of oval structures that measured about 5½ by 7½ feet and circular ones that measured about 6 feet in diameter.[10]

FIGURE 3.3. Timucua town. In this drawing by Le Moyne, thatched huts are surrounded by a palisade wall (probably palm logs), with two sentry boxes at the entrance. The text describes the palisade as "thick round pales, close together, twice the height of a man." A sentry box is "a small round building . . . full of cracks and holes," and sentinels are "men who could smell the traces of an enemy at a great distance." The large building at the town center is the chief's house, around which are houses of the principal men. The artist used one scale for the palisade (twelve feet high) and a much smaller scale for the houses. Courtesy of the St. Augustine Historical Society.

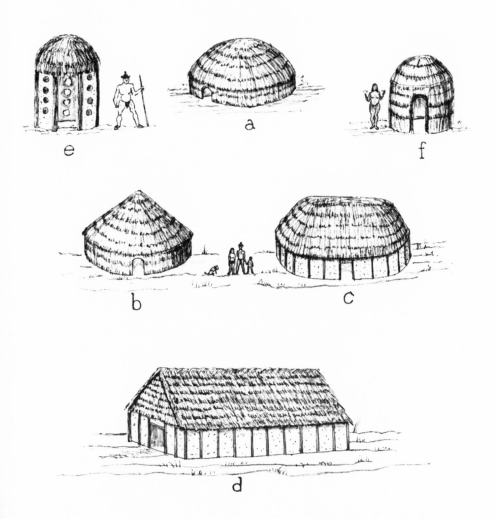

FIGURE 3.4. House types. *A:* circular plan, post and thatch, dome roof. *B:* circular plan, post and thatch, cone roof *C:* oval plan, post and thatch, wattle-and-daub walls, hip roof. *D:* chief's house and lodge, rectangular plan, post and thatch, wattle-and-daub walls, gable roof. The rectangular structure depicted by Le Moyne differs from documentary descriptions of lodges and chiefs' dwellings elsewhere along the coast. Menéndez found himself in a lodge that "could easily contain two thousand men." Fr. Andrés de San Miguel, bound for St. Augustine after shipwrecked on the northerly coast, stayed in three Indian lodges, each larger than the one before and each dome-shaped and "built of whole pines . . . joined at the top like the ribs of a parasol." *E:* sentry box, circular plan, post and thatch, wattle-and-daub walls, dome roof. *F:* seclusion, storage, or cooking hut, circular plan, cane and thatch, dome roof. Courtesy of the St. Augustine Historical Society.

Supporting the archaeological evidence is Le Moyne's overview of a Timucua village (figure 3.3); that drawing is the main basis for the house-types sketches used in figure 3.4. The exception is the small cane-and-thatch hut (figure 3.4f), which I recorded in Spain's Badajoz Province.[11] The thatch on that well-built little shepherd's hut was wheat straw, not palm fronds. Otherwise it has the characteristics of a sixteenth-century Timucua structure. Kathleen Deagan has pointed out that "archaeological evidence at the FOY [Fountain of Youth] Park site indicated that small outbuildings would have been present. . . . Documentary and analogy sources suggest seclusion huts for the ill, for menstruating women (who were required by custom to use a separate fire), as storage areas, or as separate cooking areas."[12]

For a better understanding of how the Timucuas built the structures that Le Moyne pictured, we need to examine similar housing found today in Spain, Mexico, and the Caribbean. Basic methods have not changed. Le Moyne's art testifies that dome-roofed, circular huts were majority housing for the Timucuas, and archaeology's postmolds tend to confirm Le Moyne's view. Figure 3.5 details a circular plan sill, posts, and plate (basic wall construction); figure 3.6 illustrates dome-roof framing.

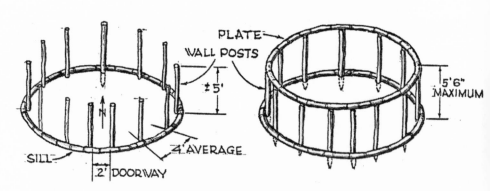

FIGURE 3.5. Circular plan—sill, posts, and plate. This hut requires flexible materials for the sill and the rafters. The sill, while not essential, is useful: its canes are curved into a circle and tied together with vines. Average diameter: sixteen feet. Posts are four feet apart, butts set into the ground against the inner face of the circle. The plate, like the sill, is a cane circle. It is secured to the tops and posts. If the posts have forked tops, the plate is laid into each crotch and lashed in place. Otherwise a pair of splints at the top of each post will serve as a crotch.

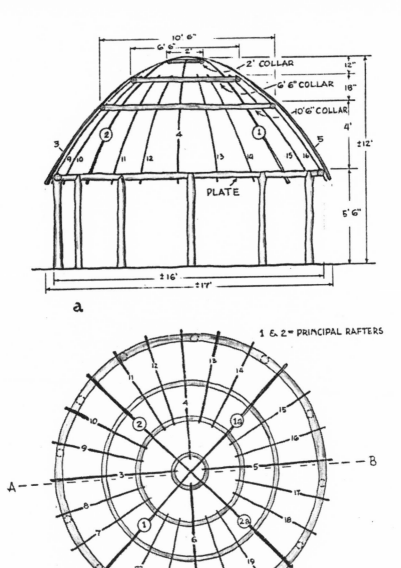

FIGURE 3.6. Circular plan—dome roof. *A:* section at AB. *B:* plate and rafter plan. The principal rafters (1, 1*a* and 2, 2*a*) are cypress poles thin enough to bend into the arch needed for the roof. The tops of each pair are lashed together. Ropes tied to the butts will pull the poles into the required arch, then the butts are lashed to the plate. The curved rafters meet in the center of the circle, and to them are lashed three circular purlins, or collars—a small one at the top center of the dome and the larger ones below it. Next come rafters 3, 4, 5, and 6, which extend from plate to the top collar. Last are common rafters 7–22; they reach from plate to the middle collar.

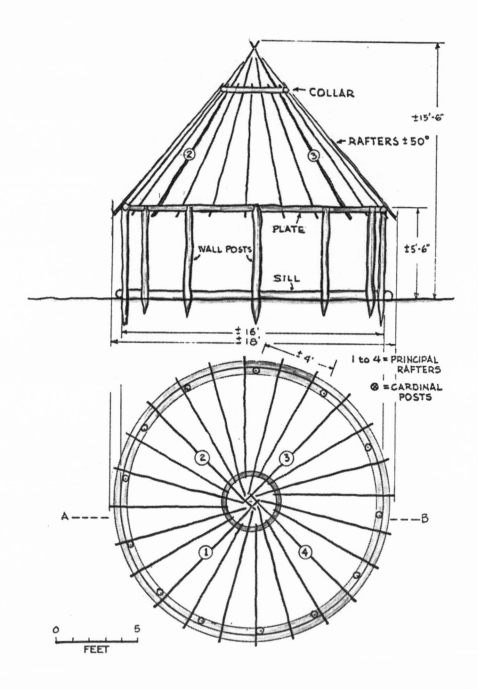

FIGURE 3.7. Framing the cone roof. *A:* section at AB. *B:* plate and rafter plan. All rafters are notched near the butts to fit snugly over the plate (see Fig. 10, *A, C*). The four principal rafters meet at the peak. Their tops are laid across each other, slightly off-center to give mutual support (see Fig. 10, *B*). A collar located about two feet below the peak supports the ends of eight common rafters and twelve short ones.

It is doubtful that any of the houses in the Le Moyne drawing have cone roofs, but because such roofs are still to be seen in the Caribbean, I include them as possibilities in Florida too (figures 3.7 and 3.8).[13]

The Indians did not have iron nails to hold their frameworks together, but they did not need them. They tied wooden members together using native plants to make the necessary cordage (figure 3.9). One of the best sources was Spanish bayonet (*Yucca gloriosa* and *Y. aloifolia*): its leaves yielded fiber that could be braided into strong ties.[14] Poles or canes, lashed across the rafters horizontally, were the supports for the thatch material, which in the St. Augustine area was the leaves of the cabbage palm (*Sabal palmetto*).

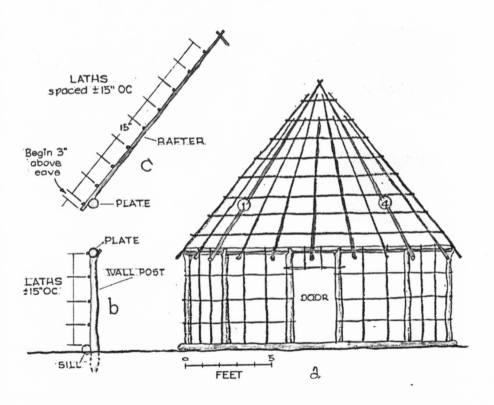

FIGURE 3.8. Laths for thatch. *A:* front elevation showing placement of laths on walls and roof. *B:* lath spacing on post and plate. *C:* lath spacing on rafter.

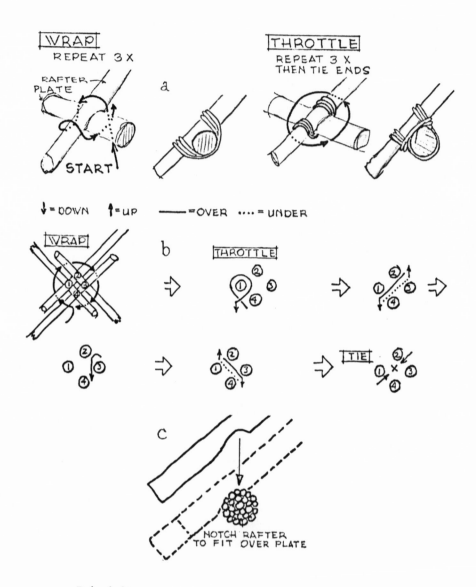

FIGURE 3.9. Rafter lashings. Instructions: *A:* wrap and throttle rafter to plate. *B:* wrap and throttle rafter peaks *1, 2, 3,* and *4. C:* notch rafter to fit plate.

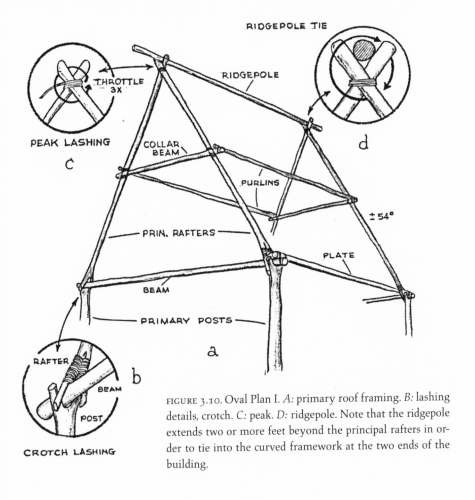

FIGURE 3.10. Oval Plan I. *A:* primary roof framing. *B:* lashing details, crotch. *C:* peak. *D:* ridgepole. Note that the ridgepole extends two or more feet beyond the principal rafters in order to tie into the curved framework at the two ends of the building.

The most complicated of the village homes (except possibly the chief's lodge) was the oval plan structure, but even it is simple if taken one step at a time. Figure 3.10 pictures the basic central frame. Figure 3.11 shows the roof framing, including the oval ends. Both drawings detail the lashings that hold the frame together.

For an oval plan building, additional secondary posts will be needed for the end curves and to give the end plates needed support. Such posts may be only 2 to 3 inches thick; their laths, 1 inch. Some thatchers prefer to place each lath on a free-standing rack at shoulder height. They hang the palm fronds on the lath,

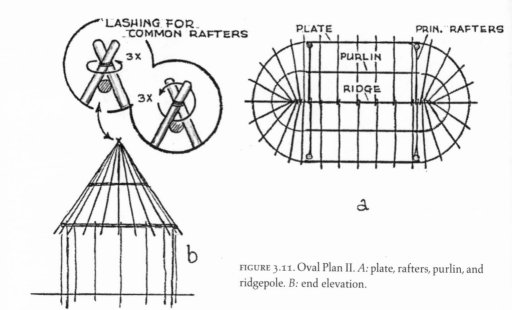

FIGURE 3.11. Oval Plan II. *A:* plate, rafters, purlin, and ridgepole. *B:* end elevation.

then take the lath with its fronds and lash it to the hut framework (figure 3.12).[15]

Thatch around a doorway needs protection from human abrasion. A bundle of small canes, preshaped into an upside-down "U," converts the doorway into a small arch, typical of the huts represented in the Le Moyne drawings. I found this arch in Spain on a shepherd's hut.[16]

Perhaps the most commonly used wall material was thatch, but there were others. In the Caribbean, with its tropical weather, one sees primitive huts with "curtain" walls of slender poles. Such walls admit every breath of air while providing a bit of privacy. Figure 3.13 illustrates vertical pole walls. These could have been used in Florida.

Archaeology indicates that hut floors were simply earth, compacted underfoot. In the center of a one-room dwelling was a hearth, which was the cooking and warming area. It was up to 6 feet in diameter, with a shallow central fire pit about 2 feet wide and perhaps a small trash pit. Against the hut walls were benches, under which there may have been little smudge pots to minimize insect presences.[17]

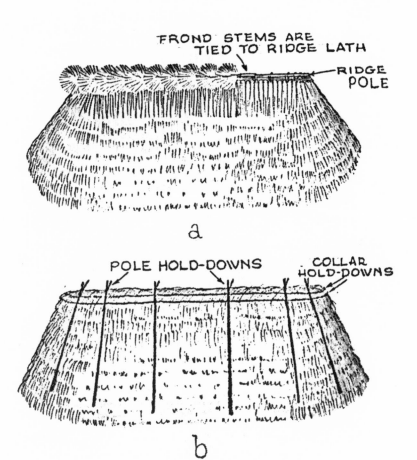

FROND STEMS ARE
TIED TO RIDGE LATH

RIDGE
POLE

a

POLE HOLD-DOWNS

COLLAR
HOLD-DOWNS

b

FIGURE 3.12. Oval plan roof thatch. Instructions: *A:* ridge cap fronds are laid parallel to and on top of the ridgepole; on each frond is left a foot and a half of the stem for tying the frond securely to the pole. *B:* cap fronds are close together and held down tightly over the ridge by continuous collars of canes or vines; these collars must be anchored by pairs of vertical poles lashed together at the ridge and extended down to the eaves.

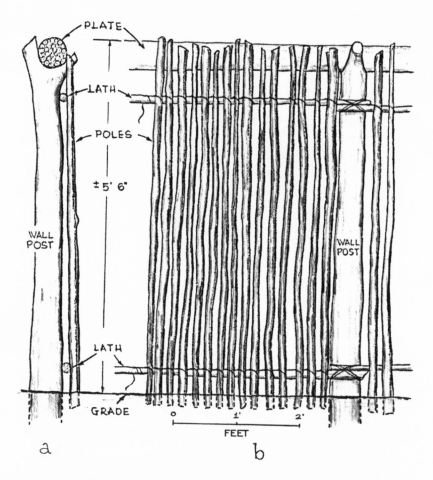

FIGURE 3.13. Vertical pole wall. *A:* section; the sill is omitted because the poles that form the wall are pushed directly into the soil; two laths are needed, one near the top of the poles and another near the foot. *B:* exterior elevation; the poles are secured to the laths with a spiral-wrapped vine or cord.

The bench or bed that I illustrate (figure 3.14) is based on two sources: my camping experience years ago and my discovery of an identical piece of furniture in a Spanish shepherd's hut. Basically the unit is a 2 foot by 6 foot backless seat or cot, supported 2 feet above the ground by short poles. The seating/sleeping surface (figure 3.15) is a cane mat.[18]

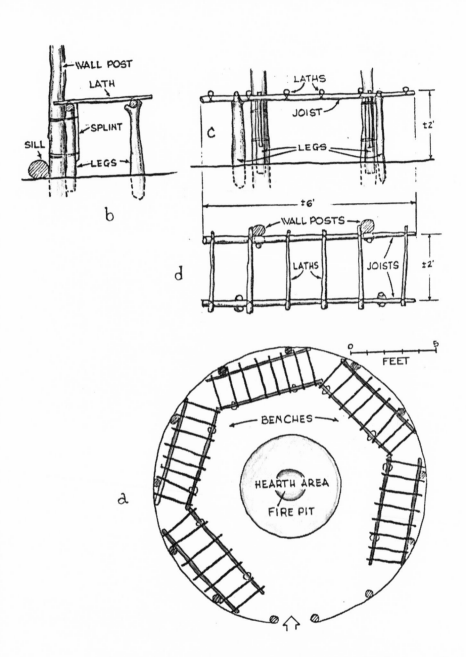

FIGURE 3.14. Floor plan and furniture. *A:* floor plan. *B:* bench or cot, end elevation. *C:* bench, side elevation. *D:* bench, plan.

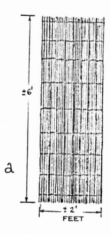

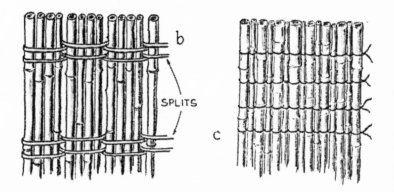

FIGURE 3.15. Cane mat. *A:* aerial view of mat. *B:* mat formed with cane splints. *C:* mat bound by cords.

The food-drying rack (figure 3.16) also is borrowed from Le Moyne, although I have omitted the Timucua kneeling to fan the fire under the rack, as well as the fish, snakes, deer, dog, and baby alligator laid upon the rack for preserving in the heat and smoke. Le Moyne's comment: "I suppose this stock [was] to be laid in for their winter's supply . . . as at that time we could never obtain the least provision from them."[19]

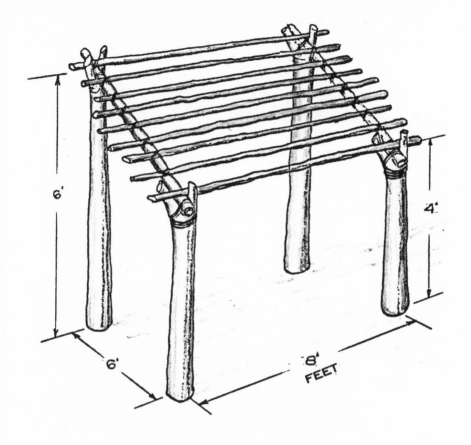

FIGURE 3.16. Food-drying rack. With a fire smoking beneath it, the rack was a means for preserving meats and other provisions. Courtesy of the St. Augustine Historical Society.

THE FIRST fragile shelters and defenses of the Spaniards lasted only eight months. While Menéndez was elsewhere exploring Florida and establishing the Santa Elena colony at the site called Parris Island in South Carolina today, the Seloy Indians went on the warpath. Their fire arrows burned half of the Great House, a barracks, and a storeroom. Bartolomé Barrientos, a contemporary, described the situation:

At St. Augustine they had twice shot arrows into the sentries on guard during the night and had succeeded in killing two soldiers. They burned the powder magazine, which readily caught fire because it was thatched with palmetto leaves. Fire arrows were showered on the houses at night whenever a breeze was blowing. The sparks caught, and nothing could stop them. . . .

The natives conducted their warfare in this wise: small groups lay in ambush to shower arrows on any stray Spaniard looking for palmetto shoots or shellfish. . . . They are so sure of not being caught that they venture very close to the Christians before discharging their arrows. These arrows are loosed with such force that they pierce any clothing as well as coats of mail. So quick are the Indians in releasing the arrows that they can wait for a harquebus to be discharged at them (when the Spaniards use these weapons), and then release four or five arrows in the interval during which the soldier reloads his piece. . . . The only way to make them keep their agreements— and they are great liars and traitors—is to rout them out of their villages, burn their dwellings, cut down their plantings, seize their canoes, and destroy their fishways. Then they realize they must do the Christians' bidding, or abandon the land.

The natives at St. Augustine and San Mateo are very treacherous and deceitful, especially since they feign friendship with

*the Christians for their own immediate ends. If they are not
given food, clothing, iron axes, and other presents when they
come to the forts, they leave in a great rage, go out on the warpath, and kill any Christians they encounter. Thus it has come
about that despite ostensibly peaceful relations they have killed
more than 100 soldiers.*[1]

When Menéndez returned to San Agustín in 1566, he and his
captains decided to leave the Seloy site and build a new fort on
Anastasia Island, at the harbor entrance across the bay. There the
Indians would be less able to do them harm and the cannons could
prevent the entry of enemy ships. With as many as 160 men working, the new fort was defensible within ten days. But there was
not room enough for all twenty cannons. Some of them were
buried to avoid possible capture by enemies.[2]

No archival drawing of the second fort has come to light, so I
have used as an example a sketch (figure 4.1) of a later fort built
on the mainland. Many of its features are no doubt similar to the
short-lived structure of 1566. For example, the moatlike excavation encircling the fort supplied earth for the fill under the cavaliers on which the cannons are mounted and for the firing steps
behind the palisades.

A word about the "cavaliers," which later evolved into "bas-
tions": Pedro de Lucuze defined them in 1772—"The cavalier (*ca-
ballero*) is an elevated battery on the terreplein (deck) of a fortification. It is located wherever it is needed. Its main purpose is to
command and dominate any part of the field."[3]

Unfortunately, the site of the second fort was claimed by the
ocean. Inspector Alvaro Flórez and acting governor Menéndez
Marquez decided that a new fort had to be built a hundred feet
away from the water. It was done in July 1566, a bit inland from
its predecessor and the angry Atlantic. A cavalier from the earlier
fort was salvaged and rebuilt into the third fort.

These were hard times. A garrison mutiny destroyed this fort
in 1570, and despite a remarkably sympathetic letter from acting
governor Pedro Menéndez Marquez (who was away at the time),
the mutineers abandoned San Agustín in October.[4]

Years later Alonso de Alas wrote the king that "when this country was settled by Adelantado Pedro Menéndez, it was for many
years on the island opposite, at the entrance of the harbor. It was

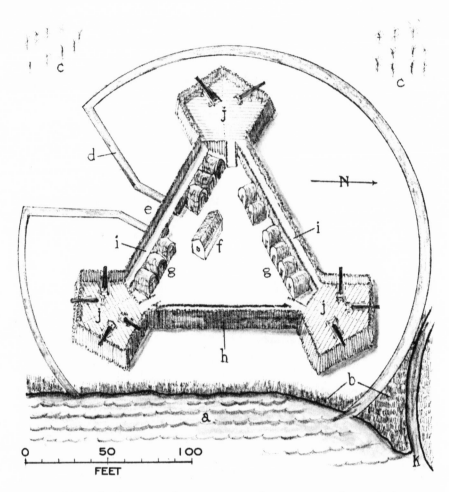

FIGURE 4.1. Triangular fort, pictured on a 1590s map of St. Augustine. The standard triangular plan was probably used for several of the early fortifications, including the second and third forts. A: Matanzas Bay. B: marsh. C: cornfields. D: borrow pit to supply earth fill for the cavaliers (gun platforms) and firing steps. E: entry gates. F: commandant's quarters. G: soldiers' quarters. H: palisade walls. I: firing steps. J: cavaliers. K: creek leading to Indian village. Courtesy of the St. Augustine Historical Society.

called San Agustín el Viejo. And because the sea ate away a large part of the island where the town and fort were situated, it became necessary to remove them to the mainland" (map 4.1).[5]

Back on that mainland, Diego Maldonado and the garrison built the fourth fort some distance south of the first fort. In 1576 it was inspected by Baltasar del Castillo, who sent a plan of the struc-

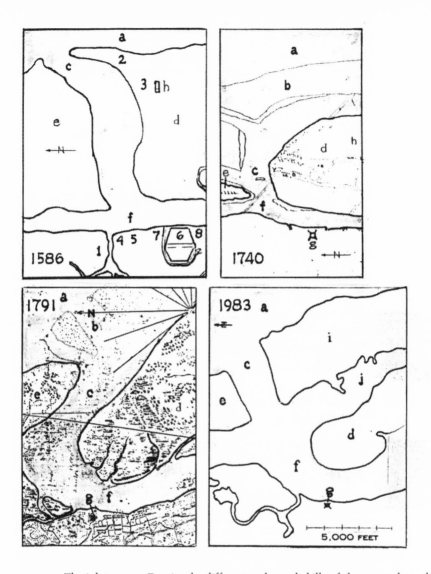

MAP 4.1. The inlet moves. Despite the different scales and skills of the mapmakers, these four maps show the radical changes of St. Augustine Inlet during the past four hundred years. Geographer John Dunkle has documented similar changes at the south end of Anastasia Island—changes that indicate that Atlantic Ocean currents and storms have pushed many Florida inlets southward. The 1983 map, however, shows an inlet now somewhat stabilized by jetties, and a 1920s seawall protects the north end of Anastasia Island (*D*). Nevertheless, beach erosion persists. The approximate sites and dates of the nine wooden forts are shown by numbers: *1:* Seloy, 1565; *2:* 1566; *3:* 1566; *4:* 1571; *5:* 1579; *6:* 1586; *7:* 1586; *8:* 1596; *9:* 1653. Names: *A:* Atlantic Ocean; *B:* Sandbars (shoals); *C:* St. Augustine Inlet; *D:* Anastasia Island; *E:* North Beach (Vilano); *F:* Matanzas River; *G:* Castillo de San Marcos; *H:* watchtower on Anastasia; *I:* Conch Island; *J:* Salt Run. Courtesy of the St. Augustine Historical Society.

ture to the king with word that Lieutenant Governor Gutierre de Miranda was working hard to get it into condition. One thing he did was to dig up the cannons that had been buried on the island and mount them in the new fort.[6] There was definitely emergency use for this fort. In 1577 the Indians were up in arms again; soldiers and colonists—men, women, and children—found refuge in the fort.[7]

Useful as this fort was, another inspector, Alvaro Flores, and Gov. Pedro Menéndez Marquez in 1578 agreed on changes for the fifth fort, which was built in 1579 behind the 1571 fort. By 1584, however, the five-year-old fort was beginning to rot. "It is nothing more than . . . a storehouse for mice," Gutierre de Miranda wrote to the king.[8]

Rot, a mutiny, and mice had brought down five forts in succession, but in 1586 it was an armed enemy that destroyed the sixth, known as San Juan del Pinillo (figure 4.2). Sir Francis Drake, coasting northward after his successful Caribbean raids, discovered the unsuspected little Spanish settlement.

Drake had two thousand men in his forty-two-vessel armada. San Agustín's population was about three hundred. Drake burned the fort and the town. The people fled to the woods and stayed there until Drake was gone.[9]

Walter Bigges, one of Francis Drake's men, described the fort:

We found it built all of timber, the walles being none other but whole mastes or bodies of trees set vppe right and close together in manner of a pale [fence] without any ditch [moat] as yet made, but wholly intended with some more time, for they had not as yet finished all their worke, having begun the same some three or foure monethes before: so as to say the trueth they had no reason to keepe it, being subject both to fire and easie assault.

The platform whereon the ordnance [artillery] lay was whole bodies of long Pine trees, whereof there is great plentie, layed a crosse one on another, and some little earth amongst. There was in it thirteene or fourteene pieces of brass ordnance [bronze cannons], and a chest vnbroken vp, having in it the value of some two thousand poundes sterling by estimation of the Kinges treasure, to pay the souldiers of that place who were a hundred and fiftie men.[10]

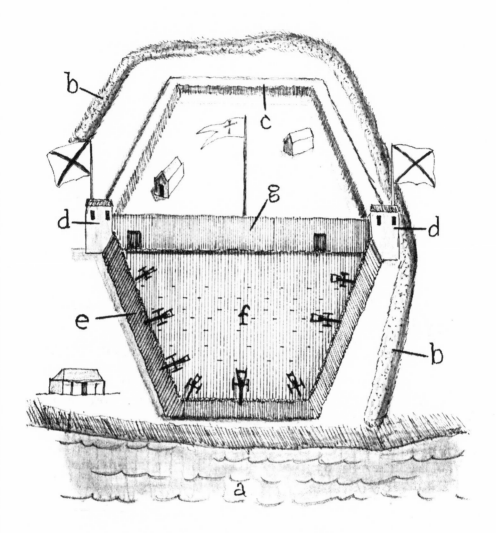

FIGURE 4.2. The sixth fort, 1586. This fort was called San Juan del Pinillo, according to Baptiste Boazio, mapmaker with Drake's armada. *A:* Matanzas Bay. *B:* moat (borrow pit for earthworks). *C:* earthwork. *D:* watchtowers. *E:* pine palisade. *F:* gun platform (cavalier). *G:* quarters(?) or ramp(?). Courtesy of the St. Augustine Historical Society.

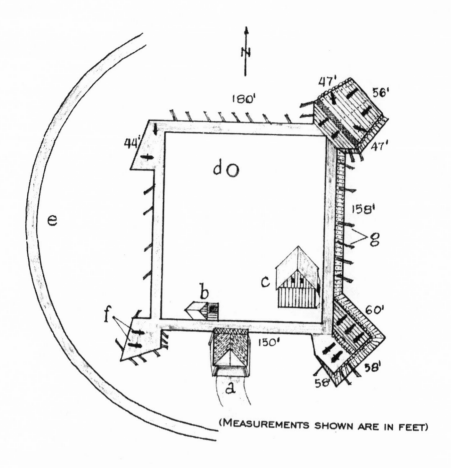

FIGURE 4.3. The seventh fort. Called San Marcos, this fort was built after Drake destroyed San Juan del Pinillo. Eight or nine years later a map informed the king of the fort's poor condition: the palisade stood only because thirty-two props held it up. The two western cavaliers, especially the northwestern one, were badly damaged, as the plan shows. The dimensions of the fort were stated, but the draftsman paid little attention to measurements. By so doing, perhaps he was emphasizing the poor condition of the structure. My drawing adheres to the stated dimensions, which make the fort almost a square. *A:* south entrance. *B:* guardhouse. *C:* quarters for the governor of the fort. *D:* well. *E:* borrow pit that supplies earth fill needed in construction. *F:* fifteen cannons. *G:* wall props. Courtesy of the St. Augustine Historical Society.

FIGURE 4.4. The eighth fort. This fort is a *casa fuerte* (strong house). It housed military personnel, weapons, and supplies. It is a timberframe structure with board walls and floors and an oyster shell tabby roof. A six-cannon battery on a raised platform covers the northern and eastern approaches, and cavaliers on the northwestern and southeastern corners of the casa have loopholes for muskets and embrasures for cannons. Each cavalier has a sentry box on its roof, and a tall watchtower stands in the center of the eastern battery. Courtesy of the St. Augustine Historical Society.

Again a fort was constructed, this one the seventh and called San Marcos (figure 4.3). Like the others, according to a 1595 report, it was

entirely of wood, propped up by 32 supports. . . . All of it is in danger of collapsing, inside and out, and it is on the site of the one which is marked for the new fortification, 140 paces nearer the town. The guns on its walls are not to be fired because it is feared all the curtains [walls] will tumble down.[11]

Its successor, again of wood (figures 4.4 and 4.5), went down before a different enemy when in 1599 a storm flooded the fort and town. It demolished houses, the guardhouse, and the storehouse with its supplies, and it swept away the fort wall and the cavaliers on the sea front. Repairs were made, but in 1631 the governor wrote the king that the fort was "defenseless and idle, being built of . . . timber which rots easily and is so dry and ready to burn that merely by using the artillery therein, fire breaks out in many places."[12]

Halfway into the seventeenth century, a new wooden fort once again defended San Agustín, this one located on the future site of the stone Castillo de San Marcos. Demolition of that old structure would be no problem for the builders of the stone fort. The inspectors reported: "We visited the old fort which is very demolished and without defense; the terrepleins, falling down, have propped the wooden framework, very old and all of a quality that needs much repair, as likewise [is] the misery of this garrison, never before in such extremity."[13]

FIGURE 4.5. *(facing page)* Eighth-fort floor plans. *A:* main gate. *B:* gun platform that commands the harbor with six cannons. *C:* site of watchtower. *D:* southeastern cavalier that serves as guardroom, with stocks and chains for prisoners; two cannons defend against attackers from nearby forest. *E:* soldiers' quarters, with bunks along the inner wall; two stairways give access to upper floor. *F:* food storage; rations were issued here. *G:* munitions. *H:* northwestern cavalier; it has cannons to defend approaches from town and forest. *I:* rectangular "windows" serving as embrasures for cannons. *J:* triangular openings that are loopholes for harquebusiers. *K:* commandant's office and quarters. *L:* officer's quarters. *M:* accountant's quarters. *N:* ensign's quarters. *O:* meeting place for city council.

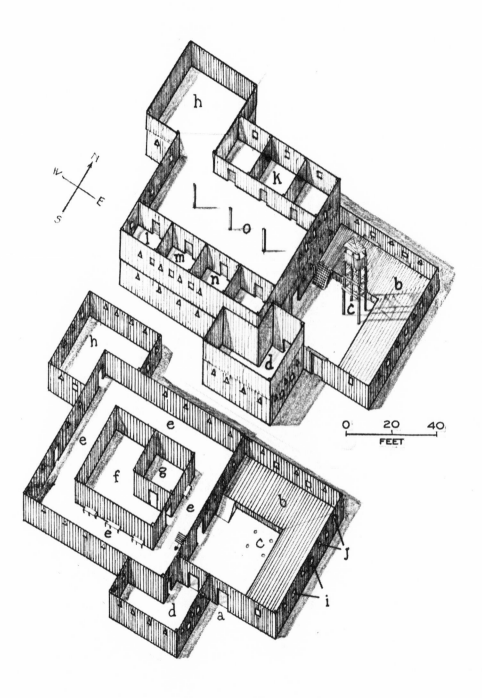

As the forts rose and fell, San Agustín's people, set down in a hostile environment unfit for farming or stock raising, beset by poverty and hunger, survived only by hard labor. An anonymous writer described the community as he saw it in the 1570s:

San Agustín where the fort and people now are . . . is almost an island, surrounded by water except for one part where they can pass to the mainland. . . . It is three or four leagues long and narrows down to half a league and even less in some places. Each year the sea covers much of this land. It is all a forest of evergreen oaks, pines and palmetto, so filled with roots that it cannot be cultivated, except a part that is sandy. There they sow maize; the governor has most of this land and makes the soldiers sow there for himself. [See comment 1 below]

In San Agustín there are thirteen married settlers, besides the soldiers, some of whom are married. Each settler will have as much land as a medium-sized garden—about what one man can dig with a hoe; just enough so that he is busy half of each day grinding the maize to eat that day. It cannot be kept ground or cooked for another day, [yet] to grind it each day by hand is hard, continuous labor.

They plant only maize and squash because other garden seeds do not yield well. Each settler sows twelve and fifteen and up to twenty pounds of maize and no more; although once, they say, one sowed forty or fifty pounds. No more is sown because of each one having only a hoe and being obliged to hand-grind the food every day. Neither is there anything that can be done, nor does the land have the capacity for yield even if more work and industry be put into it. [See comment 2]

On the small island [Anastasia] where the fort was at first, which is next to where it is now, there are about fifty head of cattle. They are of no use to the people or soldiers, nor are they killed for eating except when the governor wants one. These fifty head do not increase. If they get ready to multiply, the calves die for lack of food and because of the many big horse-flies and mosquitos there, and the bears and lions. They have no fresh water for the stock to drink except when it rains. There are about fifty hogs and these too increase little. They have been disappearing and will die due to not having food nor fresh water, and the bears and lions eat them. They have not been useful except when the governor would kill one for himself sometimes. They have gone and are wandering in the woods, so lean they are useless. . . .

There is no land for raising stock—no other animal nor flock of sheep nor goats nor any other that can be eaten, so the people have to eat only what they fish. They raise few hens, on account of not having [enough] maize to feed either them or themselves. These chickens eat small molluscs; consequently they taste fishy. [See comment 3]

The fort is [built] of planks with thick timbers for supports. It lasts four or five years, by which time the timbers are rotted by the damp earth and its saltiness. The soldiers repair it; they work all year on this fort and houses for the governors and other houses. Despite all this, many months they do not give them rations nor pay; so, beset by hunger and nakedness, they have wanted to leave. But because they have no way to go by land nor ship to go by sea, they have not gone. When they do get rations, they are not given what his majesty orders. Half a pound of meal is given; and as they come in, tired from work and have to grind and cook the food (because they do not have anyone to do it for them), they have a bad time of it. From this ground maize or meal they make cakes to cook or bake among the ashes or cinders each time they have to eat.1 [See comment 4]

COMMENT 1

The San Agustín peninsula was (and still is) covered with oaks (*encinas* and *robles*), pines (*pinos*), and palmettos (*palmas*). More specifically, *encina* can be translated as live oak (*Quercus virginiana*), *roble* as myrtle oak (*Q. myrtifolia*), *pino* as slash pine (*Pinus elliottii*) or loblolly (*P. taeda*), palmetto as cabbage palm

(*Sabal palmetto*) and saw palm (*Serenoa repens*).[2] Saw palmetto, with its sharp, rigid, curved spines on its leafstalks, is the most abundant native palm wherever there is room for it to grow. Myrtle oak, one of the smaller evergreen oaks, though stunted and wind-shaped in exposed coastal sites, grows to forty feet in protected locations.

The forest floor was so matted with root growth that planting was impossible, said the observer. Unfortunately, there is no suggestion as to the extent of the clearing that was done in the course of building the settlement in its post-1572 location. Given the hard work, time, and manpower required for clearing land, however, it is unlikely that the town site would have been denuded of forest growth for a number of years.

COMMENT 2

There was a clearing where corn was planted, and some settlers had medium-sized gardens. Most probably the clearing was an old Indian field, which served as the town commons for communal planting. It was here, rather than on town lots, that the settlers had their medium-sized gardens, although smaller kitchen gardens in town also must have existed where there were wives and the extra energy to care for them.

COMMENT 3

Stock raising was limited to cattle and hogs that were kept on the island. For various reasons, they did not thrive. The truth of this statement for its period is supported by a contemporary (1576) source that certifies that although sheep, goats, calves, hogs, and chickens were imported as early as 1567, most were butchered for food. Some livestock was taken to the island; goats were corralled and herded outside town; chickens were apportioned among the people. The source further states that native game and fish were available and essential.[3]

COMMENT 4

Heavy timbers in the fort construction rotted after four or five years of exposure to wet soil. Those timbers were the posts that anchored the timber walls of the forts.

ლ ლ ლ

Committed to the mainland after their Anastasia experiences, the
Spaniards laid out a site about a mile south of Seloy, its rectangular regularity conforming to the royal town plans decreed decades
earlier for all Spanish colonies. Drake's 1586 attack on San Agustín
destroyed the fort and the town, as depicted in Baptiste Boazio's
aerial-view drawing of the English fleet and English soldiers at-
tacking the fort and the town. Beyond the inlet and Anastasia was
the fort, and to the south was the settlement (map 5.1).

The Boazio map of 1586 is the earliest discovered so far showing St. Augustine's rectangular blocks—the same eleven-block
nucleus that exists today. The map also shows houses within the
blocks, but the scale is too small to read. Almost two centuries
later, when in 1763 England acquired Florida by treaty, Elixio de

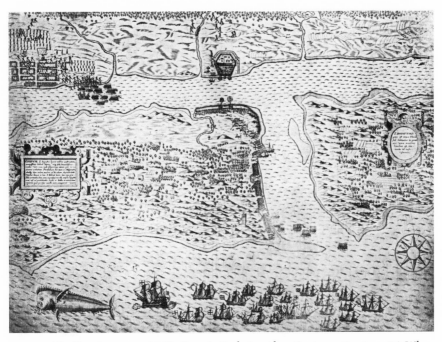

MAP 5.1. The Boazio map, 1586. Sir Francis Drake's raid on St. Augustine in 1586. When
Baptiste Boazio drew this map of Drake's attack, the fleet and the forces were his important
elements. Today Boazio's delineation of the little town serves as the earliest record of the
eleven blocks that are still a nucleus of twentieth-century St. Augustine. Courtesy of the St.
Augustine Historical Society.

la Puente prepared the official Spanish transfer map, showing the fort, streets, blocks, lots, houses, and owners. The eleven blocks on Boazio's 1586 map were included. In 1923 Goold Butler did a detailed map of St. Augustine, including the same eleven blocks.

ᐧᐧ ᐧᐧ ᐧᐧ

Not long after Drake's attack, and when the town had been rebuilt near its latest fort, another map (map 5.2) of the location was drawn in the 1590s. It centered on that fort and also pictured five buildings and two Indian villages. It was probably the work of Ens. Hernando de Mestas, who had been sent to Spain by Florida's governor to petition for funds to build a replacement for the fort.

Map 5.2 depicts the triangular fort, a small part of the town, nearby Indian villages, forests, marshes, and waterways, all drawn in considerable detail. The fort has a four-sided cavalier (raised battery) on each angle. The circular defense around the fort is a moat—a barrier that would furnish soil for earthworks to strengthen the fort.

A stockade (map 5.2h) stretches along the bay shore from the fort to the town. At the town a pier (map 5.2w) juts out into the bay, close by the guardhouse (map 5.2l) with its alarm bell on a scaffold in front. The guardhouse (figure 5.1) has eight cannon, three of them aimed over the stockade toward the bay.

Near the guardhouse are two other large buildings: the general's house (map 5.2j) and the church (map 5.2k), which has its own bell tower. Two, or perhaps three, small Spanish houses are also in the picture (map 5.2m and figure 5.2). All of these structures have vertical board walls, gables, and thatched roofs. Hold-downs are laid over the thatch at intervals. They consist simply of two poles with their upper ends crossed over the roof ridge.

The *casa de general* (map 5.2j and figure 5.3) has an outside stair to a balcony at the gable, with entry to the garret via a door in the gable. I have seen similar features in Spain's Basque provinces, which suggests that either the general or his carpenter was a Basque.

The church (map 5.2k and figure 5.4) at the north end of town near the guardhouse was probably the parish church, Nuestra Señora de los Remedios. It is similar to the church shown on the Boazio map of 1586 (map 5.1 and figure 5.5), a rectangular struc-

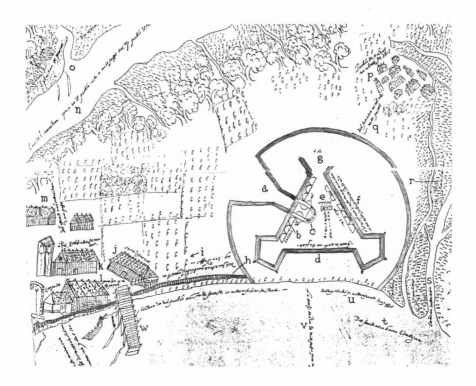

MAP 5.2. The 1590s map. Translation of the Spanish information: *A:* the fort; *B:* soldiers' quarters; *C:* commandant's quarters; *D:* length of fort's curtain: 80 feet (Spanish foot = 11 inches); *E:* soldiers: 108; *F:* each curtain wall is the same length as each cavalier (bastion); *G:* torn paper; *H:* the town stockade to the fort, with a terreplein; *I:* from the fort to the town of San Agustín: 500 paces; *J:* general's house; *K:* church may be altered; *L:* guardhouse with eight cannons; *M:* from San Agustín to San Sebastián creek: 2,000 paces; *N:* San Sebastián Creek, which circles the town; it is 1,000 paces from the town to the river above; *O:* San Sebastián of Yaocos; *P:* Nombre de Dios (God's Name), an Indian town; *Q:* from the fort to Nombre de Dios: 1,000 paces; *R:* marsh; *S:* Saturiba Creek; *T:* from the fort to the bar: 1 league; *U:* from the Isle of Pines to the fort: 500 paces; *V:* width of the river: 1,000 paces, more or less; *W:* pier; *X:* Matanzas River; this river goes to Matanzas Inlet, leagues from the town; it has two tides, one at this (south) part of Matanzas and the other at San Agustín. Courtesy of the St. Augustine Historical Society.

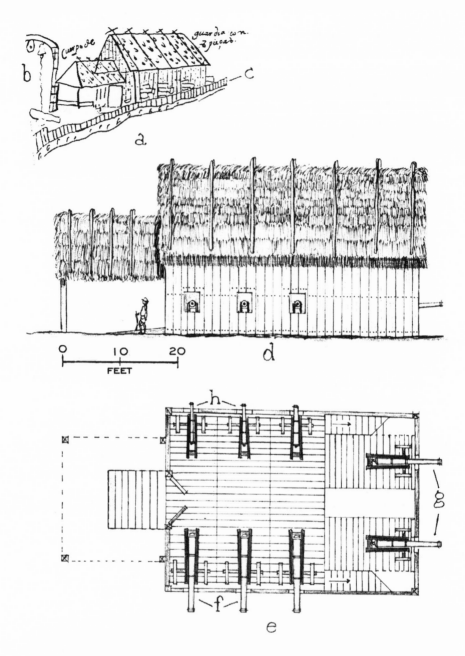

FIGURE 5.1. The guardhouse. *A:* map sketch. *B:* alarm bell. *C:* stockade. *D:* eastern elevation, vertical board walls nailed to timberframe; palm thatch gable roofs with pole hold-downs. *E:* plan showing entry ramp, interior gun platforms, and stairways to the garret. *F:* half-culverins on field carriages. *G:* sakers. *H:* half-sakers.

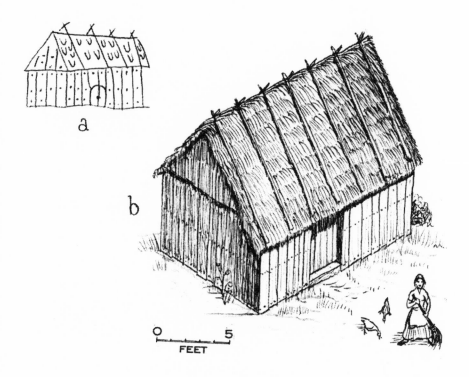

FIGURE 5.2. A settler's house. *A:* map sketch (the arched entry is not right for a board-walled house). *B:* interpretation of the sketch: single story, vertical board walls nailed to timberframe; gable roof with palm thatch and pole hold-downs.

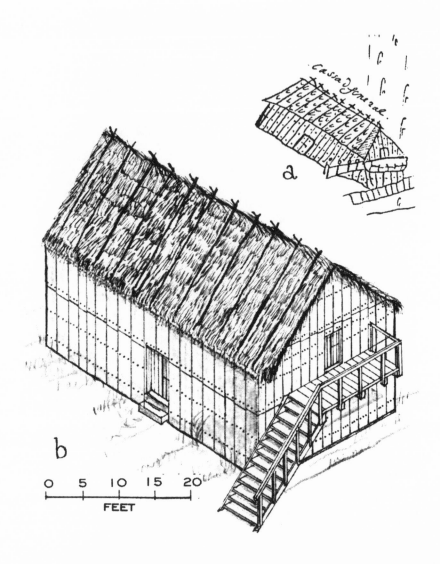

FIGURE 5.3. The general's house. *A:* map sketch. *B:* interpretation of the sketch: two-story, vertical board walls nailed to timberframe; ground floor entry in south wall; outside stairs and balcony to second-floor eastern entry; gable roof with palm thatch and pole hold-downs.

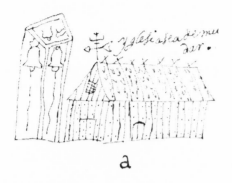

a

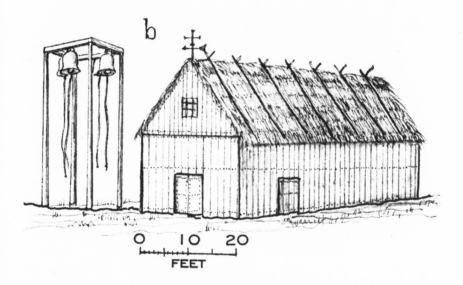

b

FIGURE 5.4. Church and bell tower, 1590s. *A:* map sketch; the text above the drawing translates to "church may be altered." *B:* interpretation of the sketch: construction is timberframe with board walls and palm thatch roof; the cross at the gable peak appears to serve also as a weathervane.

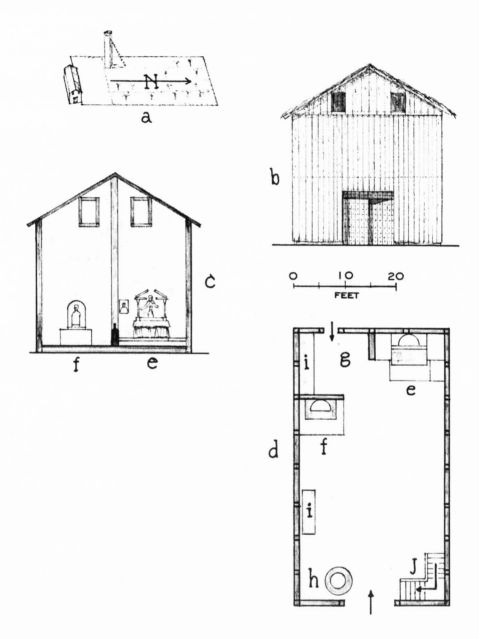

FIGURE 5.5. Church, 1586. *A:* detail of the Boazio map, showing the church and watchtower in a cleared area at the northern end of town. *B:* eastern facade interpretation. *C:* section and *D:* floor plan based on church at Balerma (Almería). *E:* main altar. *F:* altar. *G:* sacristy. *H:* holy water font. *I:* benches. *J:* stairs to choir loft. Courtesy of the St. Augustine Historical Society.

ture also just north of town (timberframe with thatched roof and board walls), which probably was burned during the Drake attack.[4]

Two Indian villages are shown on this map: Nombre de Dios (Name of God) (map 5.2s), near Saturiba Creek, one thousand paces west of the fort; and San Sebastían de Yaocos (map 5.2o), on the far shore of San Sebastían Creek, two thousand paces from San Agustín. Nombre de Dios (map 5.2p) is represented by eleven structures: eight of them rectangular, two circular, and one possibly oval. Six have thatch walls; five others could be wattle and daub. Roofs are palm thatch: five are domes, five are hips, and one may have gables. All doorway lintels are arched. No building is identified, although four display crosses on their roofs. The central structure resembles a haystack with a door, but it may be the traditional lodge or meeting place.

San Sebastían de Yaocos has seven buildings, including one that I cannot explain. Omitting that one, there are three circulars and three rectangulars, all with thatch walls; and three cone roofs, two hips, and one gable—all thatch but with only one visible holddown. Each cone roof bears a cross at its peak.

The map shows not only marshlands and forests but also farmlands. Between the town and the fort the mapmaker has plotted nine rectangles that represent cornfields planted by the settlers. Several fields may be around Nombre de Dios, but at Yaocos no fields are shown. Perhaps the mapmaker ran out of space.

ﾟ ﾟ ﾟ

The little town shown in the map from the 1590s appears also in the colorful words of Father Andrés de San Miguel, who with his companions was shipwrecked some 20 leagues north of San Agustín in 1595. His narrative of the long overland journey to reach this haven is one of the most detailed observations recorded for this period. I translate some of his descriptions:[5]

In this first [Indian] town we were lodged two days in a great circular lodge [jacal; figure 5.6], built of whole pines that lacked only the branches. The pines, poorly debarked, were set upright in the ground, and the tips all joined at the top as a pavillion, or as the ribs of a parasol. Three hundred men can sleep in it. All around the inside it has a continuous bed [cadalecho], well suited for many men to rest and sleep [figure 5.7].

Because there were no [bed] clothes except some straw thrown underneath, the door of the lodge was so small that we had to stoop to enter. All [this was] done to counteract the cold which we felt at night, and to sweat without clothing it was enough to cover the doorway at night with a door they made from palm for this, and to burn two torches inside. With only this, we were sweating at night and not feeling, being inside, the day's cold.[6]

At the next town, the Spaniards found the cacique and his head men in a "large, clear plaza, at the door of a lodge [jacal] altogether similar to the first one [described above], but larger." The visitors were well received and watched a game played in the plaza for their entertainment. Later they and the head Indians went into the lodge where they noted an idol facing the door. As in the first lodge, they sat on a circular bunk against the wall and about

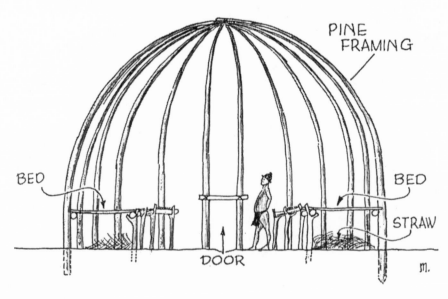

FIGURE 5.6. The Big Lodge (*jacal grande*). Pine-tree trunks were lashed into a dome and thatched with palm leaves. Father Andrés reported that three hundred men could sleep in this lodge. Courtesy of the St. Augustine Historical Society.

FIGURE 5.7. Sleeping bunk. "The *cadalecho* [bunk] was raised more than a yard from the ground," wrote Father Andrés. The fleas could not jump that high. Courtesy of the St. Augustine Historical Society.

a yard above the ground. Here they witnessed the black drink ceremony.[7]

Upon arrival at San Agustín on May 16, 1595, Father Andrés noted that

The town and presidio of San Agustín is founded on an open slope, facing east, on the shore of a clean, clear river. The town is half a league wide and one league distant from the sea. The soil is sandy and so light that it cannot support a shallow well: at all the houses they have to line them with barrels, one upon the other up to three or four, because the [ground] water is not deep and is sweet, although the sea water enters the river.

All the walls of the houses are wood and the roofs are palm [thatch], the principal ones of boards. The fort is wood and terrepleined. Now they have told me they have built a small room of lime and stone in the middle of it, brought at much cost, for keeping the powder in it. . . .

On the river banks are many and very large cypresses, from which the Indians make large canoes. . . . The Spaniards make the walls of their houses with this red cedar [savino] because the part of it in the ground does not rot.[8]

At San Agustín the castaways were warmly welcomed and quartered among the soldiers—not in barracks but in houses occupied by comrade groups. San Miguel described his pleasant stay with one such group of four *compañeros:* a sergeant, a squad corporal, and "two honest soldiers."[9] All of the town's citizens were soldiers, he said, most of them unmarried. Males born here (they were few, he noted) were given a soldier's place as soon as they were strong enough to fire a harquebus. The number of places totaled three hundred, and, except for one gunner's position, they were all filled.

During their stay the castaways were allotted soldiers' rations: 1½ pounds of flour (*harina*) daily and dried beef (*tasajo*) when it was available. The good father's ration was collected by his soldier hosts, who also kneaded the dough and cooked the meal, "which they knew how to do well, and they did it with much care." When the time came to leave, he was touched by the concern of his hosts in baking his flour ration into a plentiful supply of hardtack (*biscocho*) for the journey to Havana.[10] In fact, Father Andrés remarked on the abundance of food, except for meat:

> *I saw in this town some grapevines and fig trees, and they yield well. Also there is an abundant yield of good melons, watermelons and squash and other garden stuff; and from here they send onions to Havana (although they are not very large). . . .*
>
> *Visible to the Spanish from another part of the river is a small island of trees and palmettos, and on it some few of the king's cattle. There are no others in all the land.[11]*

His enjoyment of San Agustín came not only from pleasant association with his hosts but from not having official cares or duties and being free to fish all day if he chose to do so. He described various local fishing techniques in considerable detail (figure 5.8). There were, he wrote, plenty of fish and oysters, and "clams as big as your fist."[12]

❧ ❧ ❧

Indian building practices had evolved from time-tested use of the land's special resources, and for the Spanish newcomers there was much to be learned from the aboriginal builders. This was especially true in the selection and use of unfamiliar materials and in coping with the insect population and the climate. Unfortunately, this learning process is undocumented except in rare instances such as Father Andrés's narrative, wherein he comments on such curiosities as the framing and use of the great lodges, and the admirable qualities of cedar and cypress for construction of dwellings and canoes.

Father Andrés's description came nine years after Drake's destruction of the town, and it is clear from his narrative that the San Agustín of 1595 was considerably different from the settlement seen by the observer in the 1570s. The site was more open.

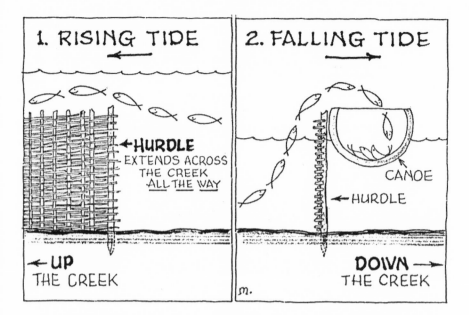

FIGURE 5.8. Fish trap. Father Andrés loved to fish and described his soldier friend's technique: "We went in a canoe up a narrow creek with a hurdle of reeds. I stayed in the canoe and wove the reeds lengthwise. As tide fell, the fish came downstream again and bumped into the reeds, or jumped over them—especially the mullets. Some fell into the canoe, but many passed on." Courtesy of the St. Augustine Historical Society.

What in the 1570s was called a "forest filled with roots" was now "an open slope . . . on the shore of a clean, clear river."

Both writers describe the gardens, one deprecatingly and San Miguel with praise for their abundant yield: melons, watermelons, squash and other vegetables, including enough onions to export. Figs and grapes also grew well, but there is no mention of citrus. Father Andrés does not mention cornfields, perhaps because he spent so much of his time fishing and enjoying the abundance of seafood. Both men remark on the unproductiveness of stock raising.

The observer in the 1570s was unspecific about house constructions (except to say that soldiers had to work on them), but Father Andrés made two significant statements: "All the walls of the houses are wood [*de madera*] and the roofs palm [thatch], the principal ones of board [*de tabla*]"; and "The Spaniards made the walls of their houses with this red cedar wood [*savino*] because the part of it in the ground does not rot." These are positive statements. By his time all house walls were wood, and the wood was cypress. Part of it was "in the ground," which means vertical boards nailed to horizontal framing, as shown on the maps from the 1590s. Earlier thatch walls had disappeared.

There was a little "lime and stone" magazine mentioned by the father. Although the discovery of shell stone (coquina) in the area came some years earlier, about 1580, this powder magazine in the fort is the first known record in Spanish Florida of stone masonry—that is, stone walling laid in lime mortar. Lime production, given the locally abundant shell deposits, must have gotten under way quite early in the evolution of the colony, even though the earliest date of record thus far is 1580. Documents of the period cite only two lime products: whitewash and roof slabs of tabby, a sort of masonry. No doubt there were others.[13]

THE EARTH

Clean sand was always available in open areas, and in the marshes clay tidal sediments were (and are) more than 40 inches deep. This marsh clay was used mainly for daub on wattle-work walls, but archaeology has found an early clay floor also, and legal documents have testified that clay was excavated from the marsh to build an oven in 1576.[1]

THE WATERS

Oysters living in the waters of Matanzas Bay and other estuaries were not only edible but a preferred food for Indians, judging by the size of the shell middens found near the villages. The Spaniards burned the shells into lime. Like the Indians, they also enjoyed eating oysters (as do present-day citizens).

THE FOREST

Pines, cedars, and palms grew profusely on the San Agustín peninsula (and still do). Cypress prefers freshwater ponds and lakes or rivers; and those are not far away. The predominant pine was longleaf pine (*Pinus palustris*). With a diameter of two or more feet, the straight trunk could reach 120 feet. Slash pine (*P. elliotti*) grows to 100 feet. But pine logs in contact with the soil as posts or sills rotted after a few years, and in the succession of wooden forts at San Agustín maintenance was a problem.

On the other hand, both cypress and cedar woods are rot resistant. The old observers called both of them red cedar (*savin, sabina, sabino*). Today these words have latinized names. Bald cypress (80 to 130 feet) is *Taxodium distichum*; it prefers deep swamps, where access and hauling were problems. For those reasons, the smaller (25 to 50 feet) pond cypress (*T. distichum* var. *nutans*) may have been preferred.[2]

Florida's red cedar (*Juniperus lucayana*), also called West Indies juniper, grows to 50 feet and was probably the *sabina* used in sixteenth-century San Agustín. But some of the documents may be recording cypress, even though they name it sabina. In the 1590s the Franciscans contracted with carpenters Juan Alvarez and Juan Gómez de Toledo to work on the forest shore to make posts and planks for the monastery church.[3] To my mind, trees "on the shore" were probably cypress, though both cedar and cypress were available.

POSTS AND PALISADES

Pole lumber is construction timber *not* worked into rectangular shape. Poles formed the basic structures in Indian building. The same was true for early Spanish housing in Florida because its use certainly required fewer hours in the preparation of materials. Nevertheless, specific references to pole lumber are few. The following is from Bigges's account of Sir Francis Drake's attack on the fort in 1586:

The walles being none other but whole Mastes or bodies of trees set vpright and close together in manner of a pale. . . . The platform whereon the ordnance [cannons] lay, was whole bodies of long pine trees, whereof there is great plentie, layd acrosse one on another, and some little earth amongst.[4]

In other words, this fort had palisade walls, and a mattress of pine logs and earth formed the gun platform. A pale is a pointed stake used for fences by being "driven into the ground" and also the fence itself, according to Webster's. In 1578 similar materials, *pinos gruesos y tablones* (stout pines and planks), were produced by the sawyers at San Agustín and sent to the Santa Elena colony.[5]

WALLS

The first colonists were faced with the need for emergency housing. They quickly became familiar with the Indian structures, and sometimes the Indians helped them build their homes. The Timucua technique involved planting a few posts in a circle; weaving walls of branches, canes, or reeds between the posts; then plas-

TABLE 6.1. Wooden elements used in Spanish and English houses

Spanish	Size	English	Size
Pilar	As needed	Post	As needed
Viga	As needed	Beam	As needed
Vigueta	6 x 6 palmos + 3 dedos	Joist	6" x 8" or as needed
Tabla	1 x 5 pies	Board	11" x 4'7"
	2 x 18 pies		1'10" x 16'6"
Tabla	3 dedos x 2½ x 36 pies	Plank	2" x 20½" x 33'
Lata o Tabla de Chilla	1½ x 4½	Batten	½" x 3"

tering the woven branches with clay. For the roof they made a palm thatch dome on pine rafters.

Architect Samuel Wilson Jr., in "Gulf Coast Architecture," cites an example of Indian plasterwork near the mouth of the Mississippi in the year 1700, as recorded by the French priest Paul du Ru: "The Bayagoula chief did the first stroke of work on the plastering, that is he began to dip moss into clay and to cover the wall with it. He did it so well that none of the others were as fast as he was." This inference is that Spanish moss (*Tillandsia usneoides*), plentiful in Louisiana as in Florida, was a major tempering material. In a later citation Wilson quotes Le Page du Pratz's description of Indian walling of "clay mortar made of earth in which sufficient Spanish moss is put. These walls have no more than four inches of thickness."

Before long, experience in producing the wooden elements used in the forts led to sawing lumber for upper-class housing—structures with wooden walls (table 6.1).[6] Sketches of these upper-class structures on the 1590s map show the walls to be vertical boards nailed to timberframe; however, the scale was too small to depict the narrow battens that sealed the cracks between the boards.[7]

The 1578 audit of the San Agustín fort noted that the southeastern cavalier was walled with heavy pine planks and the powder magazine within the fort also had board walls. Later government buildings with board walls included the customs house, the accountant's chambers, the guardhouse, the powder magazine, and a horse-powered mill for grinding corn.[8]

Thatch roofs that covered Indian huts came from "cabbage" palms (*Sabal palmetto*). The cabbage is the leaf bud at the top of the trunk that can be eaten as a vegetable—but its loss may kill the tree. (Perhaps it was that threat that caused the palms to grow so tall: 50 to 80 feet.) The leaves measure from 4 to 6 feet long. For thatch each leaf is compressed, is bound to a network of poles atop the rafters, and then functions within a bundle of tiny gutters that guide rainfall off the roof.

Palma (as the documents call it) was the primary roofing material for San Agustín in 1565, and its use persisted through the eighteenth century. Havana and South America also used palm thatch, calling it *guano*, which means "any palm tree; palm trees used for thatching; sea birds' dung used as fertilizer." A few miles north of St. Augustine is Palm Valley, named in English for its profusion of cabbage palms. South of Palm Valley flows a little river called "Guano" on some maps but now better known as the Guana River, thus avoiding the fertilizer definition.[9]

Of course, house roofs were not the only places where palm thatch was used. In 1578 a palm-thatch shed (*tejado de palma*) was built against the church to shelter barrels of flour for which there was no room in the fort storeroom. Perhaps the holy place was chosen also to discourage thievery.[10]

The problem with thatch was fire—especially if angry Indians used fire arrows, there was lightning, or sparks escaped from the hearth. Governor Méndez de Canzo lost a thatch-roofed kitchen; he replaced it with a larger one that was roofed with shingles (*tejamaniles*). In 1605 Governor Ybarra recommended to the Crown that thatch in San Agustín be replaced by wood. Perhaps that reduced the fire danger.[11] But better yet were the flat slab roofs of masonry called *azoteas*. By 1580 the Santa Elena colony had sixty houses, and thirty of them had azoteas. In San Agustín by 1603 the powder magazines, the accountant's house, Canzo's, and perhaps others had slab roofs.[12]

Masonry was possible because the colonists had learned that oyster shells (plentiful at both San Agustín and Santa Elena) could be burned into lime powder, which with shell aggregate formed rock-hard tabby, a masonry suitable for wells, roofs, and floors.

The following is from Santa Elena in 1580: "The houses were built of wood and clay, whitewashed inside and out, and with flat roofs of lime."[13]

The names of lime burners appear in records of 1580 and 1592, but production of lime must have begun some years earlier, because by 1580 the San Agustín fort had been roofed with a slab of lime-and-sand mortar (*una torta . . . de cal y arena*). Laying a roof of that extent (more than 6,600 square feet) demanded a sizable stockpile of materials. In later years, for example, forty-six barrels of lime were required for roof slabs over government quarters and powder magazines (see chapter 10).

FLOORS

In the beginning the floor was Mother Earth. She compacted nicely and did not object to having a hearth in her middle. There is also archaeological evidence that clay loam was used as flooring in early times. Kathleen Deagan described the find as 4 centimeters (1½ inches) thick. It contained two layers: the lower one was blue-green clay, roughly tempered with coquina shells; and the upper one was yellowish clay mixed with sand and crushed shells. The floor was probably clay loam of the Pellicer Series, which is dark greenish gray but grayish brown near the surface of the deposit.[14] Add fire and it turns orange-red.

Although documents tell us that tabby was used for flat roofs in the sixteenth century, the evidence for tabby floors is scanty. In 1608, however, Governor Ybarra certified that three barrels of lime were provided for flooring at the convent church.[15]

Board flooring was used in the forts and in two-story houses; it also may have been on the ground floor and in the attic. I am reminded of one early Spanish house near Avilés, Spain: It was an eighteenth-century home where the cattle were housed beneath the living room. The boards in the living room were spaced about a half an inch apart. In winter the hot-blooded cows provided heat for the living room! In other parts of Spain, where cows were not kept in the houses, the floors were board and batten, with the battens on the *under*side of the boards. (The battens were seated in notches on top of the joists.)[16]

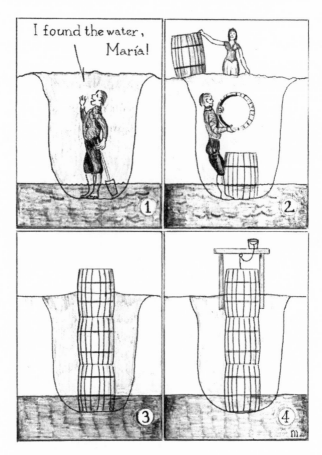

FIGURE 6.1. Barrel well.

WELLS

Food and wine came from Spain in iron-hooped barrels (*pipas*).
Once emptied, the barrels were given second careers as linings
for wells dug into Florida's sandy soil (figure 6.1).[17]

HARDWARE AND FIREARMS

Iron and lead were imported from Spain, lead to make bullets for
the firearms and iron bars to make hardware. The blacksmith ham-
mered out countless nails, hinges, bolts, and such, but he must
have run out of iron in the late 1570s: The governor had to send
to Havana for nails needed to finish the fort. Locks, if complicated, were sent from Spain.[18]

DOCUMENTS, MAPS, ARCHAEOLOGY—these reveal information about the beginnings of St. Augustine. But for the most part it is fragmentary information. Today's researcher must uncover additional resources to give depth and accuracy to the historical picture if the reconstruction of the past by words, graphics, or otherwise is to be accurate. Most important, a researcher has to *know the people.* He or she has to talk with them, walk with them, live with them—or it is impossible to *know* them. One has to experience their homes, their workplaces, and their foods.

It is true that these people have been gone for several hundred years, but one can know their descendants. What are they like? Are they really different from their ancestors? Of course they are, and yet from them one can learn a lot.

Francisco Aguilera, an anthropologist, has studied rural culture in Spain and Latin America. During the latter 1970s Aguilera was again in Spain doing field research for the St. Augustine Restoration Foundation. He recorded the number of rooms in houses and the work spaces for carpenters, blacksmiths, cobblers, tailors, cottage craftsmen, and so on—including animal shelters. He also made note of house furnishings and shop equipment. Aguilera concluded that in the villages and small towns of Spain, living and workplace layouts are essentially unchanged over the years. His findings, by documenting traditional layouts for lots, houses, and workplaces, do much to lift our concept of the sixteenth-century Spanish community above the level of conjecture.

Let me first summarize Aguilera's analysis of sixteenth-century Spain's social structure:

1. Upper class: The major civil and military powers, including nobility and wealthy merchants. They do not work with their hands, but their fingers are into moneymaking enterprises anywhere. Indoor space: Many rooms in large buildings that proclaim so-

cial position above the masses. Outdoor space: Dedication of some areas for aesthetic or recreational purposes. Not much tavern socializing.

2. Middle class: Master craftsmen, professionals, merchants—the specialists. Many of them work with their hands as well as with their minds. Indoor space: A substantial house with multiple-use rooms. Special-purpose rooms or buildings as needed. Outdoor space: Some small recreation areas; taverns and markets are social areas.

3. Lower class: Farmers, fishermen, day laborers—all work with their hands and in any labor that pays. Indoor space: Small house with multiple-use rooms for living, sleeping, work space, animal shelter. Outdoor space: Taverns for men and markets for women are social areas.[1]

With this outline in mind, we proceed to specifics for colonial St. Augustine.

☙ ☙ ☙

For most of San Agustín town lots were *peonía* size: 50 by 100 Spanish feet (44 by 88 U.S. feet). This conclusion results from map and documentary studies of 1976–77 and is supported by archaeological findings. The plot plan shown in figure 7.1, Kathleen Deagan asserts, "is found at all kinds of households in all time periods of First Spanish St. Augustine." (Dates for the First Spanish period are 1565–1763.)[2]

The typical house fronts directly on the street. At the back of the house is a detached kitchen, with a well nearby. If perchance the kitchen is in the house, then the well is near the house and close to the kitchen doorway. Sometimes there is another well or two for gardens and livestock; or if a well becomes foul, a new one is dug and the old one becomes a refuse pit. (After all, the water table is only a few feet down.) The garden, fruit trees, and shelter for the animals occupy the rest of the yard. For control of the animals there must be in-yard fences as well as the boundary fence surrounding the lot. A street gate and, if needed, a backyard gate are in the boundary fence.

In those early days families were in short supply. Most of early St. Augustine's people were bachelor soldiers. By Pedro Menéndez's ordinance they were divided into ten-man mess groups.[3]

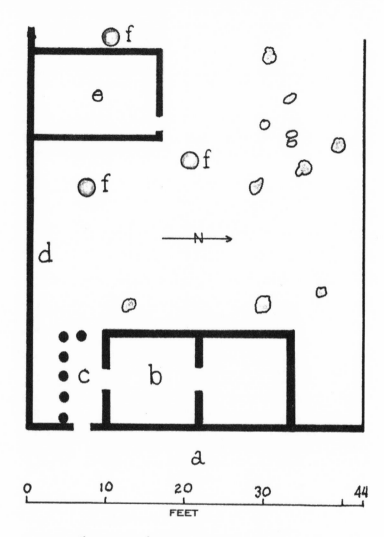

FIGURE 7.1. Characteristic plot pattern in St. Augustine, 1565–1763. *A:* street. *B:* typical floor plan. *C:* loggia. *D:* garden wall. *E:* kitchen/outbuilding. *F:* wells. *G:* trash pits. Courtesy of the St. Augustine Historical Society.

Does Deagan's plot plan fit mess groups? Presumably, yes. I have sketched several ways to provide sleep space inside a 16 by 24 foot hut (figure 7.2).

Lofts could provide overhead storage, as could shelving hung from the rafters. The personal property of an ordinary soldier was easily stowed in a small chest—for example: Miguel de Guardiola's

PEOPLE, PLANS, SHELTERS

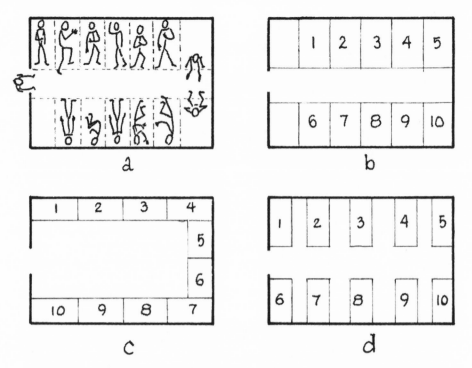

FIGURE 7.2. Floor plans for a ten-man mess group in a 16 x 24 foot hut. *A:* without beds: space for fourteen men; gear stacks against the long walls or in overhead loft. *B:* with ten 4 x 6 foot beds and 4 foot center aisle; two 4 x 6 foot areas at each side of the doorway for gear storage; storage loft can be added. *C:* continuous 3 foot bunk along three walls; with ten sleep spaces; gear goes under bunks or overhead. *D:* ten separate 3 x 6 foot bunks, 2 feet apart; 4 foot center aisle; storage under bunks and overhead. (Conjectural.)

possessions at his demise consisted of a worn deerskin jacket and a borrowed sword. More typical, however, is the inventory of Juan Ponpeyo's effects: six shirts, a jacket, an old coat, two handkerchiefs, a red bedspread, and a small *vihuela* (old-style guitar).[4] These lists include no mention of underwear, leaving us to wonder.

So the same standard plot plan could serve for mess groups. And why not two or more mess groups on the same lot (figures 7.3 and 7.4)? Among any ten soldiers there would be those with a second trade: crafts, gardens, livestock, and such; and because these activities could benefit the entire group, the plot plan may have provided them space.

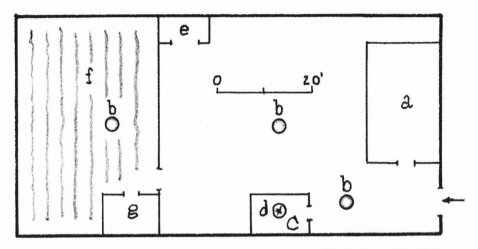

FIGURE 7.3. Plot plan for a ten-man mess group. *A:* quarters. *B:* well. *C:* kitchen. *D:* hearth. *E:* chicken roost. *F:* kitchen garden. *G:* shed. Courtesy of the St. Augustine Historical Society. (Conjectural.)

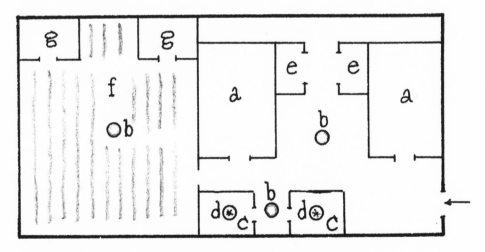

FIGURE 7.4. Plot plan for two mess groups. *A:* quarters. *B:* well. *C:* kitchen. *D:* hearth. *E:* chicken roost. *F:* kitchen garden. *G:* shed. Courtesy of the St. Augustine Historical Society. (Conjectural.)

Deagan found backyards pockmarked with trash pits. In the old days garbage was a simple problem solved by burying it in the backyard—a practice for which archaeologists are grateful.[5] Backyard disposal has persisted through the centuries. When I was a preteen lad, it was my job to dig a small pit in Grandma Evalina's backyard to inter unwanted parts of an old hen she had readied for the cooking pot. After the deposit was made I backfilled the hole. On the next occasion I dug a new hole; I never used the same one twice.

How about personal sanitation? Some three thousand years ago potential soldiers were identified as "those who pisseth against a wall"—that is, males.[6] In the ancient army recruits were instructed thus: "When the host goeth forth against thine enemies . . . thou shalt have a place also without the camp, whither thou shalt go forth abroad: And thou shalt have a paddle upon thy weapon; and it shall be, when thou wilt ease thyself abroad, thou shalt dig therewith, and shalt turn back and cover that which cometh forth from thee" (just as the cats do!).[7]

Through the ages the stable has been the civilians' latrine. All contributions therein, whether from four-legged or two-legged animals, ended on the dung heap in the yard the next day. Using barn or stable for the family outhouse still persists in rural Spain. Cartoonist José Antonio Lorigo suggested its tenacity in a sketch of a tile-walled pigpen containing a sow, two pigs, and a squatting man. A local man comes in with a visitor: "You see," he says, "we too have restrooms. And with decorated tiles, just as in Madrid!"[8]

So far, discovery of sixteenth-century latrines in St. Augustine has eluded archaeologists, leaving us to assume that: (1) local fecal deposits here were scattered and shallow, leaving no trace; (2) livestock shelters were places where both animals and humans defecated, leaving no trace because the mix of excrement and straw on the floor were conveyed the next day to the dung heap in the yard; and (3) household chamber pots, if any, were emptied on a dung heap which the chanticleers mounted each day to announce the dawn. Conclusion: A settler on his own property did not have to "go forth abroad." His lot was big enough for personal sanitation, provided his plot plan was sensible. And he could make his own digging stick, if need be.

As for the orientation of the house, according to Spanish poet Escobedo, "There is no [Florida] Indian who does not have his hut

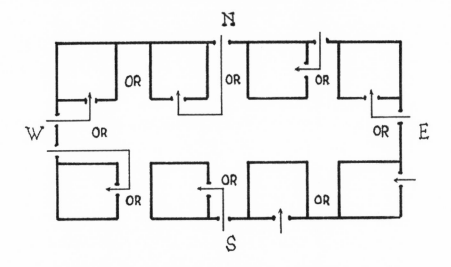

FIGURE 7.5. House orientation. Entrances can be located in the southern or eastern walls to assure privacy, shut out the winter winds, or open to spring sunshine and summer breezes. (Conjectural.)

door on the south side, for they greatly fear the north wind." And in Le Moyne's drawing of a Timucua town, all visible doorways face the same direction—presumably south.[9]

It follows that preferred orientation for sixteenth-century Spanish homes in St. Augustine put the main entry in the south or east walls, away from the chill of northerly winds but exposed to the slanting rays of winter sunshine. And in the summer, as the sun returned from its winter watch over South America, trees or arbors shaded the same south or east doorways and invited in the daily sea breeze. But how could south or east orientation be achieved when town streets run north, south, east, and west? The answer is simple (figure 7.5).

Although houses fronted on the street, not all doors were street doors. The street direction did not mandate the location of house entries. One entered the property through a gate in the street fence, and then the doorway was revealed.

Floor plans for temporary housing depended largely upon the number of occupants and their needs. Transient soldiers required few facilities other than a place to sleep and a hearth (a circular depression in the center of the hut) for warmth and cooking. Most

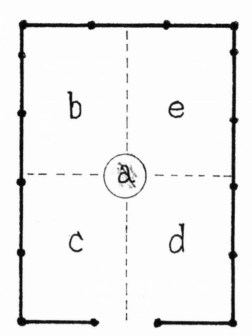

FIGURE 7.6. Fundamental areas of a post hut. *A:* hearth. *B:* sleep. *C:* kitchen. *D:* other activities. *E:* storage.

available space was for sleeping, either on the ground or on rude platform bunks (cadalechos).[10] They also needed space for stowing their chests and racking their weapons.

Nonmilitary tenants saw huts as homes, even though temporary, and could make their own floor plans. A typical plan for a one-room hut divided the rectangular space into four areas according to use (figure 7.6). As one came in the door, the hearth was in the center of the room. The kitchen occupied the near left corner; the sleeping area was at the far left. On the near right other activities (for example, eating, working, and talking) took place; the far right was for storage.

Changes were easy: Perhaps right-handed cooks wanted the kitchen on the right instead of on the left. Within the limits of available space, areas could be enlarged or diminished according to need (six beings need more sleep space than three!). And if the temporary home somehow achieved "permanent" status, it could be expanded by adding a room or two. Or a brush arbor (an arbor covered with brush cuttings) at the doorway would create more living space by providing welcome shade in the summer. Brush arbors are not uncommon in Spain today.

A grape arbor would do the same: My Grandma Evalina always had a grape arbor at the kitchen of her house. So did many of the "old folks" in her time, though I doubt they thought of them as carryovers from the distant past; they were just good to have. Grandmother's vines bore small and tasty purple grapes. Unfortunately the leaves hosted little black and yellow caterpillars that sometimes dropped upon innocent children.

⌘ ⌘ ⌘

For their temporary shelters, newly arrived soldiers or settlers would have to use materials easily at hand and quickly worked. The most likely construction would be a one-room rectangle with walls four or five feet high and a gable roof; pine, cedar, or cypress poles for the framing; and palm thatch for walls and roof. Interior dimensions would vary with the need—the smallest perhaps 8 by 12 feet, the largest probably not more than 16 by 24 feet. (The Spanish *pie* was about 11 U.S. inches.)

Such emergency shelters, perhaps more impermanent than the most humble of houses, rarely left detectable evidence of their existence except for what archaeologists call "postmolds"—impressions left in the ground by the butts of the wall posts. Unfortunately, postmolds are fugitive. Seldom do they reveal the shape and size of the structure their posts supported, because ground disturbances destroyed them or they are hiding under later construction.

So conjecture again enters the picture—conjecture based on traditional temporary structures in Hispanic rural areas. As an example, I suggest a field shelter near Palos de la Frontera (Columbus's departure port in 1492), Huelva Province (figure 7.7). The structure was about 10 by 12 feet with a doorway on the east front. There was no indication on the inside that the building was intended for anything but temporary shelter in a farm field. No doubt the dimensions were dictated by the need.

Materials for this hut familiar to the twentieth century were stalks of century plants or eucalyptus for the framing and reeds for thatch. Wall posts were 2 to 4 inches in diameter, set into the ground at 2½ to 5 foot intervals, with the tops 5 feet above the ground. Two 9 foot roof posts, with 4 to 6 inch diameters, each with a natural Y crotch at the top, supported the ridgepole, which carried 2 inch in diameter rafters about 18 inches apart. The rafters

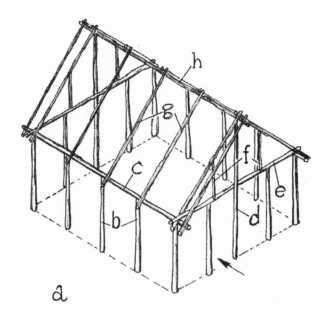

FIGURE 7.7. Spanish model. This 10 x 12 foot reed-thatch hut in southern Spain was probably similar to the smallest of San Agustín's temporary housing. *A:* primary framing. *B:* wall posts. *C:* roof plate. *D:* roof post. *E:* tie beam. *F:* queen posts. *G:* rafters. *H:* ridgepole.

were flattened at the eave for firm seating on the plate. At the roof peak each rafter pair was crossed upon the ridgepole and lashed together. Roof pitch was about 40 degrees.

Straight saplings or reed poles, 1 to 2 inches in diameter, were used for lathing. They were secured—wired, tied, perhaps some nailed—to the framing at 12 to 18 inch intervals.

The maximum diameter of the reed stems used for thatch was a quarter of an inch. The stems were tied at one end into 3 inch in diameter sheaves with tough esparto grass, then lashed by that end to the lath. A single row of curved tiles was laid on top of the roof ridge to waterproof it.

Three small openings were placed in the west gable thatching for ventilation. The doorway in the east wall was 2½ by 5 feet. The door? Plywood.[11]

In St. Augustine this Spanish model could have been used with but few changes. Pine or cypress poles would make the frame—probably pine, because it was more accessible. For thatch, leaves from the cabbage palm would be used.

Before starting to build, the boss builder looked over the site, cleared it, and made sure his building would not sit in a big puddle when it rained. With a stack of poles in hand, the workmen separated the different sizes wanted for wall posts, roof posts, roof plates, ridgepole, and rafters. Wall posts, the foundation of the framing, were about 3 to 6 inches in diameter. Archaeological evidence shows that the butts were sharpened to drive into the soil. These were primary posts, spaced about 4 feet apart on the wall lines. (Framing techniques illustrated in chapter 3 may help to clarify my descriptions.)

Pole framing needs tight joints for secure assembly. Major junctions such as roof plate to primary post were generally mortise and tenon, unless the top of the post was a Y crotch that would grab the plate naturally. The roof plates carried the weight of the roof and, like the posts, were 3 to 6 inches in diameter.

Tall posts on the centerline of the hut supported the ridgepole. A ladderlike scaffold eased the task of lifting and lashing the ridgepole atop these posts and helped in laying up the rafters.[12]

Rafter poles were in pairs, their tops crossed over the ridgepole and lashed to it. Their eave ends were flattened or notched to bear snugly upon the roof plate, then lashed.

Next came the roof laths. Straight-stemmed reeds or canes, if an inch or so in diameter, were spaced about 15 inches apart and lashed in place.[13]

Thatching began on the number 2 lath, just above the eave lath. The thatcher pointed the leaf stem toward the roof peak, pulled the outer splits under the number 2 lath, squeezed the thirds together, then tied them down to the eave lath. Thus the thatcher moved along the line, making each leaf into a sheaf beside the others. And so it went, lath by lath, each leaf compressed into a 3 or 4 inch sheaf, making the thatch about 6 inches thick (figure 7.8).

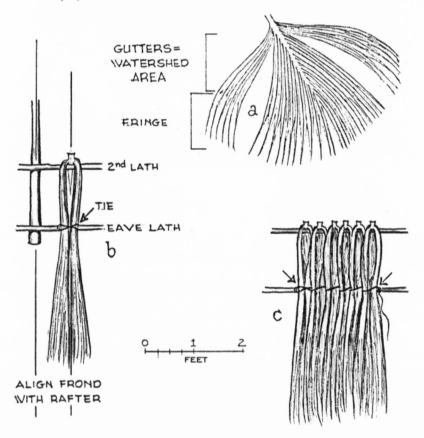

FIGURE 7.8. Thatching, the start. Fronds have natural gutters that guide water runoff. Instructions: *A:* split the frond (as shown). *B:* pull the splits apart and hook the front over the second lath; tie the frond down on the eave lath below. *C:* with a strong cord, use a spiral twist around frond and lath to bind each frond securely in place.

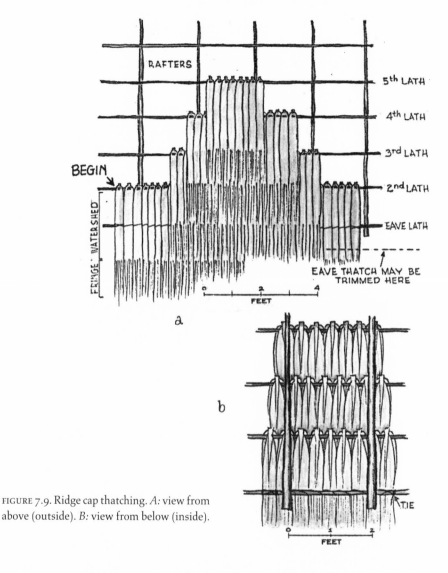

RAFTERS

5th LATH

4th LATH

3rd LATH

BEGIN

2nd LATH

EAVE LATH

FRINGE · WATERSHED

EAVE THATCH MAY BE
TRIMMED HERE

0   2   4
FEET

a

b

TIE

0   1   2
FEET

FIGURE 7.9. Ridge cap thatching. *A:* view from
above (outside). *B:* view from below (inside).

At the roof peak the thatchers needed a lath as anchor for the
ridge cap. They made a long lath by splicing two or three together,
laid it into the crotches where the rafter pairs joined, and lashed it
down. For the ridge cap, 18 inch stems were left on the palm leaves,
and these stems were tied to the ridge lath so that the leaves lay
on top of and parallel to the ridge (figure 7.9).

That done, the leaf ends fluttered upon the ridge like wings, so
the thatchers pushed them down upon the roof slopes and cap-

tured them under a pair of reed collars (or vine nets) that paralleled the ridge. The collars were anchored by pairs of hold-down poles crossed over the roof peak on top of the thatch. The downward ends reached almost to the eaves.

Now, back to the walls: Because the primary wall posts were some 4 feet apart, sometimes secondary posts were needed to reinforce the horizontal lathing that would support the wall thatch. These secondaries were slender vertical poles, their butts pushed firmly into the ground in line with the outer faces of the primary posts and about 16 inches apart. The tops were lashed to the outside face of the roof plate. Onto this frame of vertical posts went horizontal laths. The bottom lath needed a hold-down added to press the thatch leaves firmly against the ground (or sill, if there was one).

The essential openings in a temporary shelter were for access and ventilation: a doorway and smoke holes. The doorway: Two wall posts, either on the east or south side, spaced at least 2 feet apart, were the doorjambs. Sometimes a roof post was one of the jambs. The roof plate or a tie beam served as the lintel. To protect the thatch at the doorway from human abrasion, an exterior frame of boards or bundled reeds could be laid over the thatching and tied to the door frame. The door itself opened inward. It could be made of cane splits woven over a sturdy cane frame or of skins, hung as a curtain or mounted on a frame. For a light door, leather-strap hinges secured to jamb and door served well enough; but a wider, heavier door of boards needed iron hinges, such as staples or straps.

The door latch was on the inside, sometimes only a tie, sometimes a wooden bar that slid into a socket cut into or mounted on the jamb. A simple up-and-down latch could not be used unless the round jamb was severely flatted to receive it. Obviously this was not exactly a snug-fitting door.

Indian houses had no windows, according to French artist Le Moyne's portrait of a Timucua town. Yet the cooking hearths were inside, always burning. And not only the cooking hearths: Challeaux, another Frenchman, observed that "Little flies annoy them often; to get rid of these vermin they make small fires in their houses—especially under the bed." Archaeologists find those little smudge pits today on Timucua house sites at St. Augustine.[14]

One can be reasonably sure there were no windows in Spanish temporary structures, but ventilation came from small triangular openings in the gable peaks, where the top course of thatch was omitted. From these vents hearth smoke escaped and fresh air entered. Blocking the vents kept out some of the chill winter winds, or in summer kept in smoke to discourage insect entry.

In the next chapter readers will see how the typical plot plan discovered by Kathleen Deagan suited some early St. Augustine citizens.

Francisco González, native of Cañaveral, came to Florida in 1566. He was a drummer in the military and also town crier. Drummers conveyed commands to the troops by a variety of drumbeats, which could penetrate even the noisy confusion of battle. Being a professional noise maker, he was an effective town crier.

The above information is known about the man through official documents. Francisco's house (figure 8.1) is conjectural, based on what is learned through archaeology, cultural records, and general accounts of San Agustín in the sixteenth century.

He probably had an Indian wife. Her influence would be especially evident in food procurement and preparation—that is, in planting and cultivating the kitchen garden and having her own kind of cookware that she could use to prepare the food her husband would eat. After all, providing food for her family was an Indian woman's duty. I am sure that González accepted an Indian-built kitchen as readily as he took unto himself an Indian wife.[1]

So, to the standard plot plan of house, kitchen, wall, and garden there are some adjustments: Instead of a rectangular European kitchen, the lady has an oval or circular Indian one, plus a small Indian-type outbuilding for garden needs. And in addition to a hearth for outdoor cooking, over the hearth is an Indian rack for drying or smoking meats. The vegetables also have Indian ancestry.[2]

In the 1560s Francisco Camacho (figure 8.2) was both a soldier and a fisherman. He came from San Lúcar de Barrameda (Cádiz Province) on Spain's southwestern Atlantic coast, where he learned how to fish. He married Teresa, an Indian girl, and also had Catalina and Catalina's son Juan in his household. Catalina was probably Teresa's sister.[3]

With three Indians in his daily life, it would appear that Camacho liked the Indian lifestyle. Maybe he liked it well enough to per-

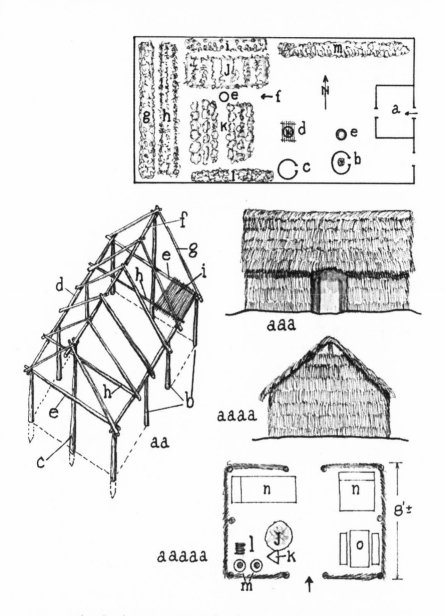

FIGURE 8.1. Plot plan for Francisco González, drummer and town crier. *A:* house. *B:* kitchen. *C:* shed. *D:* food drying rack over hearth. *E:* well. *F:* kitchen garden. *G:* beans. *H:* corn. *I:* gourds. *J:* squash. *K:* pumpkins. *L:* cucumbers. *M:* tobacco. *AA:* primary framing. *B:* wall posts; *C:* roof post; *D:* roof plate; *E:* tie beam; *F:* ridgepole; *G:* rafter; *H:* joist; *I:* loft floor (canes). *AAA:* eastern elevation. *AAAA:* southern elevation. *AAAAA:* floor plan. *J:* hearth; *K:* stool; *L:* fuel for hearth; *M:* food jars; *N:* bunks; *O:* table and benches. Courtesy of the St. Augustine Historical Society.

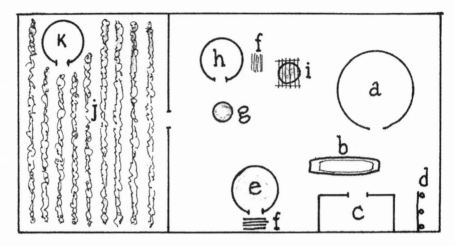

FIGURE 8.2. Plot plan for Francisco Camacho, soldier and fisherman. *A:* thatch hut (for details of round huts, see chapters 3 and 5). *B:* Indian dugout. *C:* storage. *D:* net drying rack. *E:* smokehouse. *F:* firewood. *G:* well. *H:* kitchen. *I:* hearth and food drying rack. *J:* kitchen garden. *K:* isolation hut and storage. Courtesy of the St. Augustine Historical Society.

suade Indian friends to build Indian-style quarters for him and his family. Perhaps they even gave him an Indian dugout for a wedding present!

℘ ℘ ℘

A step up from the thatch-roofed and thatch-walled houses were those with more substantial walls of wattle and daub (figure 8.3). However, homes still had the omnipresent palm thatch roofs.

What is a wattle? First, this kind of wattle has nothing to do with a rooster's chin decoration, although for some strange reason his colorful appendage and the primitive structural panel both seem to derive from the same Anglo-Saxon word, *watel.* Second, not many structural wattles can be seen today unless one goes to certain places. Wattlework is not a forgotten technique. It can be found in the Caribbean, Mexico, and many other parts of the world.[4] The dictionary defines *wattle* as "a sort of woven work made of sticks intertwined with twigs or branches, used for walls, fences and roofs."[5]

To make "a sort of woven work" more specific, picture the builder setting the primary wall posts into the ground, just as he did for the thatch hut. The primaries establish the outline of the

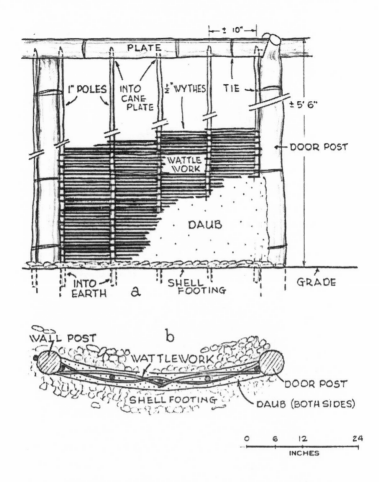

FIGURE 8.3. Wattle-and-daub wall. *A:* elevation showing the upright poles, oyster shell footing, flexible horizontals woven into the verticals, and the daub (clay plaster) over part of the wattle; the finished wall extends from footing to plate. *B:* plan showing the "wattlework weave"; the daub is on both sides of the wattle but leaves part of the wall posts exposed.

structure's outer walls. Then, along this outline, between the primaries, he sets in the vertical poles of the wattles. These have less diameter than the primary posts and are spaced about 18 inches apart, depending upon the flexibility of the wythes.

Wythes are the horizontal members of the wattle. For them workmen gather flexible willow branches, woody vines, or the like that average about an inch in diameter. These they cut into suitable lengths and interlace into the vertical framework. (In Spain hazel branches are preferred for wythes.)[6]

The verticals in wattlework must be rigid enough to withstand the pressure of the wythes without undue warping, which indicates a diameter of about 2 inches. So if the verticals are 2 inches thick and the wythes are up to 1 inch, then the wattle will be about 4 inches thick. Add the daub and you have (almost) a 6 inch thick wall. Because the wattles and wythes have thick places and thin places, it is up to the daub (and the dauber) to even things up. Do not expect the wall surfaces to be monotonously flat as in modern plasterboard.

Spain's southern coast was the subject of a "National Plan for Improvement of Fishermen's Housing" during the 1940s. The survey produced a three-volume pictorial record of existing structures, many of which were post houses with wattle-and-daub walls. However, the wattle-and-daub surfaces were quite thin, so the post construction was conspicuous. Probably at St. Augustine it was quite visible too.[7]

Wattles can be used a lot of different ways, many of which do not need daub. In the Santander Province of northern Spain I have see wattlework fences, wattle-walled sheds, and wattle partitions in barns; only one of the latter was plastered with clay. Wattles can make balconies safe or be used to build exterior walls; for gable peaks they form ventilating closures.[8] They can be found from the Basque provinces westward to Galicia and also in parts of Burgos and Soria. They are an ancient construction technique indeed, and seeing them still in Spain's ancient rural buildings can evoke thoughts of what life was like five or ten centuries ago.[9]

This mention of naked wattles does not mean that daub is absent from Spain, although in his monumental work of Spanish folk architecture Carlos Flores photographed a facade that was all naked wattlework. A few pages earlier he showed substantial wattle-and-daub walls.[10]

How were these wattles secured to the tall timberframes? In the works just mentioned, the horizontal timbers that supported wattles provided continuous slots, top and bottom, wherein the tapered ends of the wattle's vertical poles were seated. And each end of the wattle's horizontals was lodged against a vertical timberframe post. In-and-out tension held the wythes firmly against these verticals.[11]

It is unlikely that second-story wattles were used in St. Augustine. Second-story houses belonged to upper-class tenants. They preferred board walls.

So much for wattles. Now, what is daub? The dictionary calls it "a kind of mortar; plaster made of mud." And mud is "moist, soft, sticky earth, such as found in marshes and swamps, at the bottom of rivers and ponds, or in highways after rain." So, according to Webster's, daub is just mud. But for house builders, it has to be more than just mud. Mud washes away when it rains.

Archaeologists in St. Augustine have recovered fragments of orange-red daub that bear wattle impressions. It was the color of clay.[12]

To those who know the red clay hills of Georgia, the coastal flatlands of northeast Florida might seem the last place to look for clay. But not so; from a soil survey of St. Johns County, read this revelation: "The Atlantic Coastal Lagoons consist of the Matanzas River, San Sebastian River, North River, Tolomato River, and Guano Lake. This region consists of open water and flat grassy marshes that are subject to daily flooding by normal high tides. Most of the soils are mineral soils that are *high in clay and silt content*" (emphasis added).[13]

Map 8.1 shows the marshes that surround St. Augustine. To the north there are also extensive marshlands; Kurths Island marshes, for instance, are $1\frac{1}{4}$ miles long. And these sources of clay along the west shore of the river are documented by the tragic death of Luis Rodríguez in 1576. Luis and a coworker had gone up the North River to dig a load of clay. On the way back to town, a storm capsized the craft. Because Luis could not swim, he drowned.[14]

I also should mention "the clay hole." In the 1920s (and perhaps earlier too) it was a popular children's swimming hole carved out of the east bank of the San Sebastian by a wandering creek. It was about a hundred yards north of State Road 16. Big oak trees on the bank pushed their climbable limbs over the water for the daredevils who liked to dive.

And in 1960 road workers widening a section of Lewis Speedway (so named in the dear old days when 15 mph was speeding) uncovered a sizable bed of clay. Two neighborhood boys, Reggie Pamies and Michael King, saw opportunity in the discovery—not for building a wattle-and-daub hut but for advancing science and

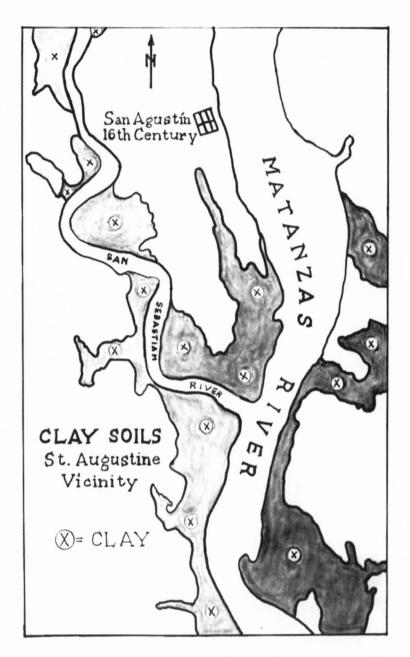

MAP 8.1. Clay soils, St. Augustine vicinity. Courtesy of the St. Augustine Historical Society.

art. With clay from the road job they sculpted dinosaurs (small ones).[15] Someday I hope archaeologists find similar art efforts made by sixteenth-century children.

What is clay? It is fine-grained earth, chiefly aluminum silicate, produced by the deposit of fine rock particles in water. So says Webster's. The soil scientists say that clay is mineral particles smaller than 0.002 millimeters. Or as a "soil separate," it is soil containing at least 40 percent of clay.

In the St. Augustine vicinity clay occurs in marshlands that formed in clayey sediments. These soils, named the Pellicer Series, occur along streams and estuaries and in tidal basins near the Atlantic coast. They are flooded daily by high tides.

The Pellicer strata may be found from 0 to 80 inches deep and are described thus:

0–10 inches: silty clay loam, dark grayish brown, slightly sticky;

10–55 inches: clay loam, dark greenish gray, very sticky;

55–70 inches: sandy clay, dark greenish gray, very sticky;

70–80 inches: sandy clay loam, dark greenish gray, slightly sticky, coarse pockets of fine sand, loamy fine sand, and sandy clay.[16]

A daub supply could be deposited, mixed, and kept ready for use in a shallow steep-sided pit dug close to the job. Trial and error showed whether "very sticky," "slightly sticky," or something in between should be used. In daubing the daub, experience helped. Daubers covered both sides of the wattle. The exterior was waterproofed with whitewash made from oyster shell lime. Most likely the inside was whitewashed too. The posts remained clearly visible.

The orange-red daub unearthed by archaeologists at St. Augustine raises a question. How did greenish-gray clay turn red? I believe the answer is fire. From the beginning, St. Augustine's thatch roofs were highly vulnerable to cooking fires, Indian fire arrows, English torches, and lightning. In 1586 Francis Drake did the most thorough job of arson, transforming gray daub to red; but there were also other fiery catastrophes, notably those in 1577 and 1599.[17]

Modern-day restorationists are seldom called on to daub mud on wattles, but they are faced with a similar problem when they plaster over wooden laths. Fortunately one learns quickly. I once was committed to plastering over a doorway (no longer needed) in Grandma's Abbott Street house. The lathwork was thin, rough wooden strips, half an inch apart, so the plaster could squeeze into and slightly out of the gaps between the laths. In doing so the plaster formed "keys" in back of the laths that anchored it in place. My first vigorous sweep pushed a trowel-full of plaster all the way through the laths. I heard it smack on the floor of the next room. My second sweep was gentle, and the plaster plopped at my feet. It took many more tries before I adjusted trowel position and vigor to produce keys in back and smooth plaster in front—both at the same time.

❧ ❧ ❧

Juan Calvo, native of Mérida (once a Roman town), in Extremadura Province, came to St. Augustine as a settler, but by 1572 he was in the military. He was also a farmer. By 1575 he was selling corn to the garrison. That is all we know about him, but I have given him a wattle-and-daub house and planted corn on his lot for his convenience, although he may have also acquired a farm lot outside the town (figure 8.4).[18]

Juan Mordazo (figure 8.5) came from Ribera del Fresno, a small town on the banks of the Valdomede River in Extremadura. He was a settler in 1568, then served as a soldier at Santa Elena during 1575–76. Back in St. Augustine the next year, he sold the government a weight set and balance, plus 712 fathoms (almost a mile) of palm cordage. The next year he sold more than 4 miles of it. It must have been good-quality stuff! Too bad we do not know any more about it except that one heated palm leaves to expose the inner fiber, then used that fiber to make anything from thread to rope.[19]

Juan de Espinosa was a soldier and part-time cobbler from Lucena, Córdoba Province. Lucena is about 30 miles due south of the capital. Espinosa's hometown is an area of row houses with masonry walls, tile roofs, and patios, but because St. Augustine was in its prestone era, he probably got along with a simple one-story wattle-and-daub house. Traditionally a shoe shop was part of the shoemaker's home. Juan has a 5 by 8 foot space at the front door (figure 8.6).[20]

Francisca de Vera was a widow, and certainly a woman of mental and physical ability in order to operate a boardinghouse in a frontier town (figure 8.7). Menéndez had his soldiers divide themselves into "comrade groups," usually of ten men. Señora Fran-

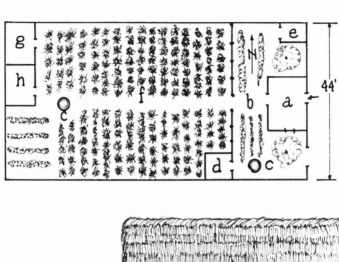

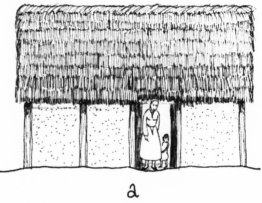

FIGURE 8.4. Plot plan for Juan Calvo, settler, farmer, and soldier. *A:* house. *B:* kitchen garden. *C:* well. *D:* kitchen. *E:* chicken coop. *F:* cornfield. *G:* shed. *H:* pigsty. Wattle-and-daub house, 12 x 6 feet: *A:* eastern elevation; *B:* southern elevation. Courtesy of the St. Augustine Historical Society.

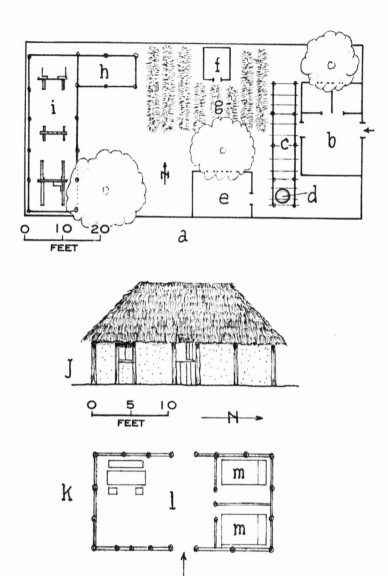

FIGURE 8.5. Plot plan for Juan Mordazo, soldier and cordmaker. *A:* plot plan. *B:* house; *C:* arbor; *D:* well; *E:* kitchen; *F:* garden storage; *G:* garden; *H:* cord storage; *I:* rope walk. *J:* eastern (street) elevation; 12 x 24 foot wattle-and-daub house with hip roof. *K:* floor plan. *L:* living/dining room; *M:* bedrooms. Courtesy of the St. Augustine Historical Society.

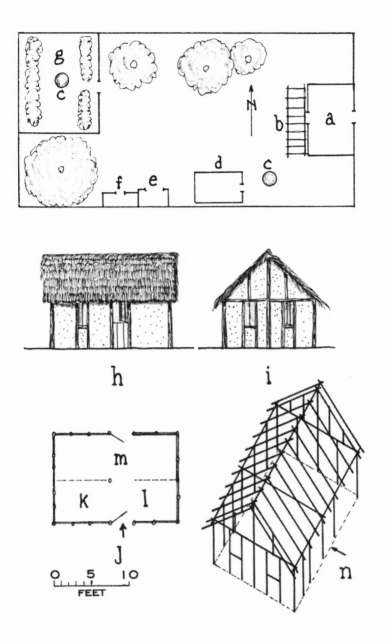

FIGURE 8.6. Plot plan for Juan de Espinosa, soldier and cobbler. *A:* house. *B:* arbor. *C:* well. *D:* kitchen. *E:* chicken coop. *F:* shed. *G:* garden. *H:* eastern (street) elevation; gable roof, 12 x 18 foot wattle-and-daub post house. *I:* southern elevation. *J:* floor plan. *K:* shop; *L:* living/dining room; *M:* bedroom. *N:* primary framing. Courtesy of the St. Augustine Historical Society.

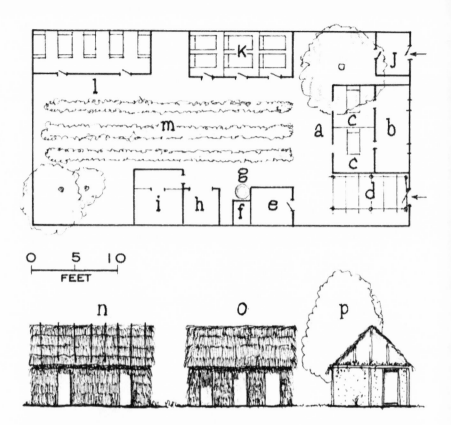

FIGURE 8.7. Francisca de Vera's boardinghouse. *A:* plot plan and boardinghouse. *B:* dining room. *C:* bedrooms for Vera and maid. *D:* arbor. *E:* kitchen. *F:* laundry. *G:* well. *H:* chicken coop. *I:* pigsty. *J:* barbershop and bedroom. *K:* bedrooms for guests. *L:* bedroom for comrade group of five soldiers. *M:* garden. southern elevation of houses: *N:* comrade group dormitory; *O:* guest rooms; *P:* boardinghouse. Courtesy of the St. Augustine Historical Society.the St. Augustine Historical Society.

cisca's comrades numbered only five, which probably meant that they were congenial old-timers. The following descriptions are documented.

Corporal and squad leader Juan López came from Avilés in 1566.

Blas Hernández joined the Archiniega fleet at Great Canary Island and also came in 1566. He was a gunner and carpenter.

Santos Hernández, from Carmona (a few miles east of Sevilla), came about 1570. He was a soldier, a sawyer, and a cord-and-rope maker.

Hernando de Segovia was from Mérida (Extremadura) and arrived in 1568. He came as a settler and barber and became a soldier but did not give up his barber business.

Miguel de Escudón was a Basque from the mountain village of Aya (Vizcaya Province). He enlisted in the Royal Armada, did not like it, and left—without permission. So he was sent to Florida in 1573 to serve three years in the military for desertion. He was also a carpenter and sawyer. Maybe the other carpenters recruited him.

Each comrade group pooled its rations and hoped that one of its ranks was a good cook. At Francisca de Vera's this group simply handed their rations to Vera and she fed them. She also operated a laundry for them.[21]

Middle-Class Homes

CHIEF CARPENTER Martín de Yztueta was from Lazcano, a Basque village in a mountain valley about 25 miles southwest of San Sebastián. Because Martín came to Florida with Pedro Menéndez in 1565, surely he was one of the twenty axmen—Basque and Asturians from the wooded slopes of northern Spain—who cleared the way through the storm-lashed forest for Menéndez and his 500 on their march to take French Fort Caroline. Later, as *carpintero principal*, Martín was responsible for carpentry in government construction.[1]

Available documents tell nothing about Martín's family, but we can be fairly sure that a man in his position had a wife and children, and also an apprentice or two. Coming from the Basque region, Martín had to be familiar with timberframe construction, from the tree-felling stage to the completion of multistory structures. It was knowledge essential for building wooden forts, other government structures, housing for the colonists—and himself.

In Martín's snowy homeland the big farm buildings called *caseríos* had everything together under one roof: stables and equipment on the ground floor, living quarters and storage upstairs, and the harvest—forage, grains, meats, and such—in the loft. When the time came, it seems likely that he would build such a structure in Florida, especially when Florida's virgin forests could—and did—provide an abundance of timber. So I drew a plot plan (figure 9.1) with a caserío-type house, a kitchen garden, a corral, and a couple of wells.

The street elevation (b) of Martín's caserío is based on a sketch by Julio Caro Baroja, noted historian of the Basque people and their architecture. His sketch records a *tipo arcáico* (archaic type) of caserío in Guipúzcoa, the home province of the chief carpenter, so the conjectural design for Martín is a two-story-plus-garret timberframe, board-walled structure. (See the appendix for illustrations of timberframe techniques used in Spain.) It has a por-

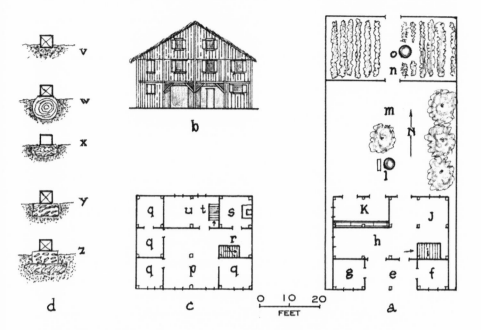

FIGURE 9.1. Plot plan for Martín de Yztueta, soldier and chief carpenter, from the Basque province of Guipúzcoa. *A:* plot plan. *B:* southern elevation of house. *C:* second-floor plan. *D:* typical foundation footings. *E:* entry; *F:* office; *G:* tools; *H:* shop; *I:* stairs to second floor; *J:* lumber storage; *K:* stable; *L:* well and water trough; *M:* corral; *N:* kitchen garden; *O:* well. *P:* living/dining room; *Q:* bedrooms; *R:* stairs; *S:* kitchen; *T:* stairs to loft; *U:* storage. *V:* sill laid on ground; *W:* sill laid on flatted cedar log; *X:* sill laid on oyster shells; *Y:* sill laid on tabby foundation (oyster shell, sand, and oyster-shell lime); *Z:* sill laid on tabby over oyster shell footing. Alex Bealer, expert woodworker, notes that cedar will last in the ground for seventy-five to one hundred years, especially if it is charred on its surface to discourage rot and termites. (Conjectural.) Courtesy of the St. Augustine Historical Society.

tico entrance that faces the street and gives access to all parts of the building: to the office on the right; to the toolroom on the left; and straight ahead to a wide door to the shop and a smaller one to the stairs for the upper floor. This entry is also a loggia, an open-sided, sociable family room, or where a cart can be pushed in, out of the rain.

The facade has eight windows, several more than it would have in the climate of Martín's homeland. The house plan (a and c) is a rectangle 30 by 39 U.S. feet, occupying virtually the entire width of the lot. In keeping with Basque tradition, the structural posts mark the four bays (compartments) that are the basis of the house plan.

Carpentry operations are on the ground floor; the shop is in the center, with lumber storage and table in the back corners. The floor might be simply packed earth, swept clean as needed; but more likely the big sills underfoot are covered with board flooring.

Three wide doors—one for the shop and two for the stable (home for the beasts that haul lumber)—are in the back wall. The stable also may be a comfort station for family and workmen, especially in bad weather.

The stair to the second floor is close to the portico and gives quick access to the living quarters: kitchen, dining room, living room, four bedrooms, and storage. The bedrooms are small, hardly more than 8 by 8 feet, but the living, dining, and storage rooms occupy two of the four bays and are quite spacious.

To reach the garret, residents would take the stair in the storage room. Once under the roof, they would find it simply open space with not much headroom. In the homeland it would provide storage for the farm produce. In Florida I doubt the chief carpenter did much farming, but the space is there, if needed. And where there is space, people usually manage to fill it.[2]

For his big house Martín needed firm foundations. At the time he was building, stone was not available. True, the existence of shell rock (coquina) was reported in the 1580s, and in the latter 1590s Governor Gonzalo Méndez de Canzo used it to build a powder magazine in the fort. Later records, however, point out that San Agustín houses "were made of wood, almost impossible to repair" (1655); "in ruins" (1655); "wood with board walls" (1675); "merely boards with palm-thatched roofs" (1680). So Martín did not use stone.[3]

On the other hand, oyster shells were available in quantity. The shells by themselves make firm foundations, but more about that later. I think Martín used them. But actually, the sill itself could serve as the foundation if it were cypress or red cedar.[4] Both of them resist ground rot, and in the sixteenth century the best bet would be either cypress or cedar sills on shell foundations.

Normally we think of sill timbers under only the exterior walls. However, Martín's support thirty-two big posts: fourteen in the exterior walls and eighteen inside (figure 9.2). The logical way to

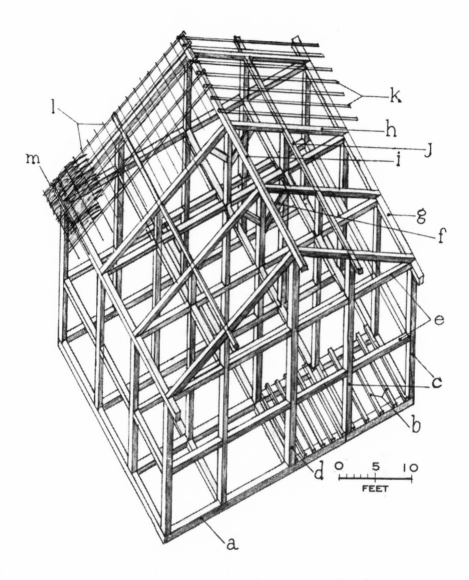

FIGURE 9.2. The Basque carpenter's timberframe house. *A:* sill. *B:* floor joists. *C:* posts. *D:* king post. *E:* tie beams. *F:* brace. *G:* roof plate. *H:* principal rafters. *I:* ridge. *J:* purlin. *K:* common rafters. *L:* laths for thatch. *M:* thatch. Courtesy of the St. Augustine Historical Society.

support the insiders is to put them on sills like the outsiders, so that there is literally a network of sills.

Remember, however, that the outside posts are singles that extend from sill to roof. They were probably longleaf yellow pine (*Pinus palustris*), a hard, heavy, durable wood from tall, straight trees growing in the forests nearby. In fact, pine, being a readily available material (though not always longleaf), is in most of the framing.

The inside posts are not long singles; they are triplets. Each of the three floors has its own set of six floor-to-ceiling posts. Ground-floor posts support second-floor beams; second-floor posts support garret-floor beams; garret posts help support the roof. All the posts are broadax-squared and tenoned into the meeting members at the bottom and top. In other words, the sill network under the building is matched on the second and garret floors by tie beams carried atop the posts. The principal beams are the exterior ones: the girt at the second floor and the plate at the eave level. But the interior tie beams are necessary too; tie beams not only connect the posts but support floor joists (which support floors) for each story. They could be mortised into the beams, but that would mean using thicker beams and a lot more work. Besides, it was common practice in Spain to omit the mortise.

Diagonal braces from post to beam (figure 9.2f) were commonly used to strengthen the joinery, especially in outer walls at corners and wide openings. Perhaps Martín would have added more braces than I have. Another common post-and-beam reinforcement was the *zapata*. This was a short timber placed horizontally atop the post as in the letter *T*. Often the ends of this 3 or 4 foot timber were decoratively shaped. T-posts were used as needed (or wanted) for exterior or interior supports, especially under beams that were spliced together at the top of the post.

Studs, the smaller verticals between posts, help to support the horizontal beams of the framing network and anchor the materials used for both interior and exterior walls. They also are located and spaced as door- and window-frame verticals for the office, toolroom, stable, lumber room, stairways, and shop downstairs, and for the quarters upstairs. There are no windows on the north exposure except at the stairways. The garret has small windows at each end.

In Spain the spaces between the studs were usually filled with cob (adobe, clay, or bricks)—forming a wall. In tree-rich Florida, however, vertical board walls gave support to the horizontal members of the house frame, and a lot of studs were not needed (figure 9.3).

What were needed were horizontal nailing strips for the boards (figure 9.3h). Sketches on the 1590s map show the vertical boards nailed to the sill at the bottom, to the roof plate at the top, and to a nailing strip in the middle, all of which means the boards were probably about 8 feet long. In other words, each floor probably had its own board wall. If so, then second-floor boards overlap the tops of the ground-floor boards. For a first-class job, these overlaps require the addition of filler strips at the second- and top-floor levels.

Longer boards may have been used for two-story houses such as the casa de general depicted on the 1590s map. This possibility emerges in documents of 1576, which record payments for production of planks 16½ and 33 U.S. feet long. But most likely such heavy lumber was for fortifications or other government constructions.[5]

That local sawyers could keep a two-man saw right on the mark for 30 feet or more speaks well of their skill. I am sure they could produce accurately cut boards for house walls or whatever. If the chief carpenter wanted smooth faces on the boards, he could put an apprentice to work with the jack plane or else call in the whitewash crew after the wall was built.

Unfortunately there is no clue as to how the builders sealed the crack between these vertical boards. In Spain, where boards are used to protect eroding cob or for loft walling, gaps between boards are commonplace. In our own New England some seventeenth-century "plank frame" houses have the spaces between the vertical boards filled with a mix of clay and cut straw. This same kind of seal might have been used at San Agustín—not so much to block out the winter cold as to exclude the rain, wind, insects, and other vermin. Of course there were other solutions: joints could be caulked, as the ship carpenter caulks the planks of a boat; the wall boards could be lapped over each other an inch or so; the sides could be linked together by rabbeting or tongue-and-groove work; or the joints could be covered by battens, a method known

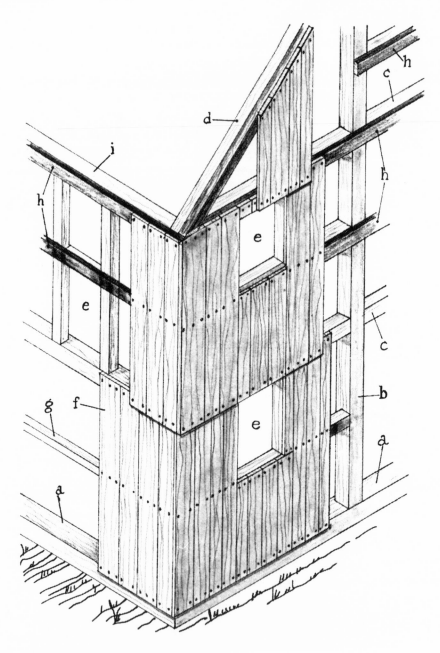

FIGURE 9.3. Timberframe house with board walls. *A:* sill. *B:* post. *C:* tie beams. *D:* primary rafter. *E:* window frames. *F:* random width board walling. *G:* nailing strips. *H:* filler strips. *I:* roof plate. Courtesy of the St. Augustine Historical Society.

to have been used in sixteenth-century Havana. The latter is the way I think Martín would do it, provided his sawyers could produce long wood strips about half an inch thick and 2 or 3 inches wide that could be nailed over the crevices between the wall boards.[6]

Sometimes floorboards also posed a problem in the old days. I studied a centuries-old upper-class home in Asturias that retained its original chestnut flooring in the second-floor *sala* (living room). Spaces between the boards were finger size. Under the sala was the dormitory/dining hall for the cows. In cold weather bovine body heat percolated through the porous floor above and warmed the sala. The trouble was, in hot weather flies ascended into the sala to cool off. In Florida I think tight joints are, to say the least, sensible.[7]

Openings (doors, windows) required studs or other verticals as framework (figure 9.4). Necessary horizontals could be mortised into these members and the doors or shutters hinged directly to the studs or other verticals (figure 9.5). Or a window frame or door frame, complete with jambs and lintel, might be set in between the studs. Doorsills, however, were omitted in much of the Spanish work I have seen.

According to my analysis of the roof slopes in the map of the 1590s, the average angle of slope was about 45 degrees. But setting Martín's rafters at 45 degrees meant the garret would have 20 feet of headroom—unreasonable! I think Martín settled for 30 degree slopes and maximum headroom of 10 feet.

The foundation-to-roof posts in the four exterior walls (see figure 9.2) are the basic supports for the rafter system. The posts on the sides of the house are capped by the roof plate (figure 9.2g), that horizontal beam which receives the eave ends of the four principal rafters. On the front and back of the house, however, the posts go from foundation all the way to the rafters, and horizontals between the long posts are demoted to tie-beam status.

The ridge plate (figure 9.2i) stretches from one to the other of the tall center posts in the gables, with in-between support from the garret's center-line king posts (figure 9.2d). The principal rafters (figure 9.2h) go from roof plate to ridgepole, with a midway lift from the garret's queen posts (the shorter ones).

Framed into the principal rafters are the purlins, those horizontal members that carry the common rafters (figure 9.2k). Up to

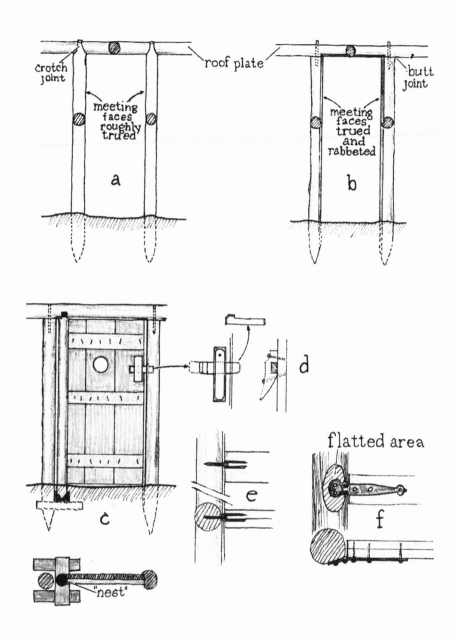

FIGURE 9.4. Post door frames and doors. *A:* simple post frame (same exterior and interior). *B:* shaped post frame (interior face). *C:* trunnion or "mare's nest" hinge. *D:* sliding bar latch. *E:* staple hinge. *F:* iron strap hinge.

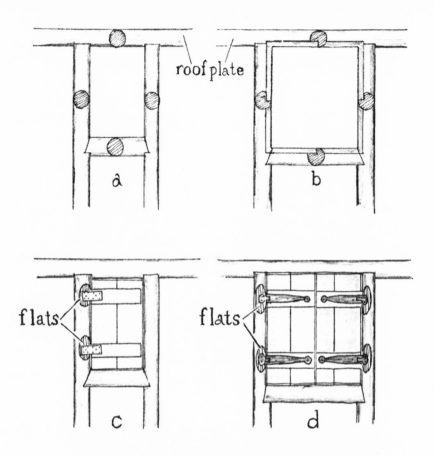

FIGURE 9.5. Post window frames and shutters. *A:* simple post frame (same exterior and interior). *B:* rabbeted post frame (interior). *C:* single-leaf shutter with leather hinges (interior). *D:* two-leaf shutter with iron hinges (interior).

this point the major posts and beams in the house were probably broadax-hewn pine; but for a palm thatch roof, cypress poles make the best common rafters. Each pair will be halved and pegged together over the ridgepole, flatted to seat on the midway purlin, and notched over the eave purlin to project 2 or 3 feet as the eave.

Then come the horizontal laths for the thatch (figure 9.2m), spaced about 15 inches apart, depending on the size of the palm leaves. I won't go into putting on the thatch, because I've explained it earlier (chapter 7).

Once you know what you want to build and how to build it, you have to figure what materials and labor you need, where to get them, and how to pay for them. Today those procedures are comparatively easy—except perhaps for the last one. But in sixteenth-century Florida nothing was easy.

Being a craftsman of experience, Martín could handle such details. Too bad he left us no record of how he did it. Still, I think we know the materials he needed:

Masonry (oyster shells, lime, sand). A 6 inch bed of oyster shells alone was enough of a foundation under the sills of his house. Better yet would be a mix of lime, sand, and shells on top of a bed of shells (figure 9.1d). Lime burners could furnish both shells and lime. And to make lime, people had to gather the shells. Fortunately the sources were not far away in middens and on the shores. A man could dig down a couple of feet in the backyard for good, clean yellow sand. And two or three feet deeper was water for the mix.

Cedar and cypress lumber. Approximate dimensions (in inches): sills, 12 x 12; principal rafters, 6 x 6; ridgepoles, 4 x 6; purlins, 4 x 4; common rafters, 3 inch poles; laths, 2 to 3 inch poles; exterior boards, random widths.

Pine. Primary beams, 8 x 8; tie beams, 6 x 8; posts, 10 x 10; studs, 4 x 6; joists, 6 x 6; nail strips, 2 x 6; interior boards, 1 inch random; battens, ½ x 3.

Cabbage palm. Leaves for thatch, trunks for posts.

Iron. Nails, hinges, latches, shutter hooks, door strips.

Getting lumber was the big problem, but in early times pine forests were right outside town. For cypress one had to find freshwater streams or ponds. They, too, were not far away.

An axman alone could fell a tree, but when he came to a giant one, he welcomed the sawyers. The man with the ax cut a deep notch about waist high on the side he wanted the tree to fall. Then the sawyers made a horizontal cut from the opposite side of the tree, slightly above the notch. When the weight of the tree began to bind the saw, they drove a wedge into the cut to ease the pressure. After more sawing and deeper wedging, the tree toppled. The next steps were to remove the branches, cut the trunk into manageable (or specified) lengths, strip off the bark, and get the logs to the workplace and convert them into lumber.

Obviously, logs and lumber were moved from place to place, but so far the documents don't tell us how, except for a hint that cypress cut in or near streams that connected with the coastal waterway may have been rafted to landings in St. Augustine.[8] When I was a kid, long rafts of palm logs from Palm Valley were common sights in the bay, towed behind tugs headed for construction of a new dock somewhere along the waterway. Rafting was a way to move lumber, but there was still the question of how to get it into and out of the water. Animal power—oxen, mules, men—solved the problem. A universal method was to lash one end of a log to the axle of two monstrous wheels behind a team of oxen or mules (or men) to haul the wheels and then drag the log or logs to the sawyers' workplace.

Since earliest times men have devised ways of lifting burdens too heavy for human muscle power. A Spanish hoist, for example, was used to lift construction materials from one level to another by means of a rope over a wheel at the top of a scaffold. One end of the rope attaches to the load; the other end runs under a second wheel at the base of the scaffold and thence to the power source: horses, mules, oxen, or men.[9]

The "sawmill" where the sawyers cut the logs into lumber (site unknown at present) was simply the place where one or more pairs of trestles (big sawhorses) were located, along with a shed for the sawed lumber. When a log was lifted and secured onto the trestle, a pair of sawyers marked the line of their first cut with a charcoal-covered string stretched tightly along the log. Snapping the string made a visible guideline along the wood. Then the pair got to work—one atop the log to guide the long saw on the mark, and the other underneath, to help supply the power needed for cutting (figure 9.6).

With straight-grained wood, expert axmen could split logs lengthwise very close to the line and faster than the sawyers could saw. And following with a good sharp broadax, they could produce smooth surfaces. They could take the roughness out of sawed surfaces too.[10]

Palm thatch. Because Florida's cabbage palm (*Sabal palmetto*) can grow to 80 feet, its leaves are often hard to reach. Fortunately,

FIGURE 9.6. Sawyers. In 1578 San Agustín had five sawyers who produced timber and boards. Their basic tool was the "pit saw," so-called because the low man worked in a pit beneath the high man, who was atop the log. But at San Agustín the water table was close to the surface, and a pit was not always feasible. The sawyers were Domingo Benito, Martín Hernández, Martín de Salterín, Santos Hernández, and Alonso Escudero. Courtesy of the St. Augustine Historical Society.

in the growing process the tall palms drop millions of seed berries, so there were (and are) within reach plenty of young trees with 4 to 6 foot leaves suitable as thatching material. In fact, these palms even provide "ladders" in the form of "boot jacks" on their trunks—stem bases that stay firmly attached for years.

Ironwork. Without iron nails, how could a carpenter build? He could use trenails (wooden pegs), which were good for boat building because water swells them into a tight bond. But on dry land iron nails were the first choice to hold wooden structures together, and in 1565 Pedro Menéndez had six hundred *arrobas* of iron (or 7½ tons) loaded aboard vessels bound for Florida. Not all the cargoes made it to St. Augustine, but archaeologists have found iron nails on sixteenth-century sites, and the factor's accounts from 1565 to 1569 list nail stocks on hand in sizes from horseshoe nails to spikes. Later imports are also on record; and right in San Agustín soldier Cristóbal Gonzáles was serving as a nail maker.[11]

The blacksmith of record was Juan Ruiz, who came to Florida about 1573. By 1577 he was selling iron bars and steel to the Crown (that is, to the king's local officials for use on government projects). His wife was Beatriz de Uzeda.[12] They were from Llerena in the south part of Extremadura Province. Across the north part of that province flows the Tajo River on its way to the Atlantic. It is a boundary between the Extremaduran north, where there was wood, and the south, where there was very little. South of the Tajo is a land of red-brown soil, rolling hills, and flatlands; of grapes, grain, groves—and few trees. Wood is scarce. The major building materials for the simple, attractive traditional homes are soil and stone. From the soil comes the clayey mud for adobe bricks and the loam for *tapia* rammed-earth walls. Stone makes walls and floors. Some stones can be calcined into lime, and lime added to tapia makes *tapia real,* a more durable version of mud wall. Furthermore, Extremaduran quality lime mixed with earth makes floors as well as mortar for stone masonry and whitewash to waterproof the walls of these shining white traditional homes.

I have not been to blacksmith Juan Ruiz's hometown, but I remember Zafra, a village of adobe, tapia, and tile roofs, just 25 miles northeast of Llerena; and Fuente de Cantos (Fountain of Songs), a charming community of whitewashed houses just fifteen miles to the west. Carlos Flores reproduces a typical plot plan of that area: in size, the lot is 32 by 76 feet, a bit smaller than the peonía lots of St. Augustine. The plan is simple. The house fronts on the street; a patio is behind the house; the kitchen is separate, at one side of the patio (Deagan's plot plan again!). A stable occupies the back of the lot.[13] Basically, that is the layout I have used for Ruiz (figure 9.7).

As Ruiz dreamed of building his Florida home, probably one of the big problems facing him was his unfamiliarity with Florida building materials, so different from the soil and stone resources of his homeland. Nor could he do all the work himself. He probably made the nails, hinges, and such, but building a big wooden house required a team of workmen: laborers, loggers, sawyers, carpenters, masons, thatchers, blacksmiths, and an overseer. In

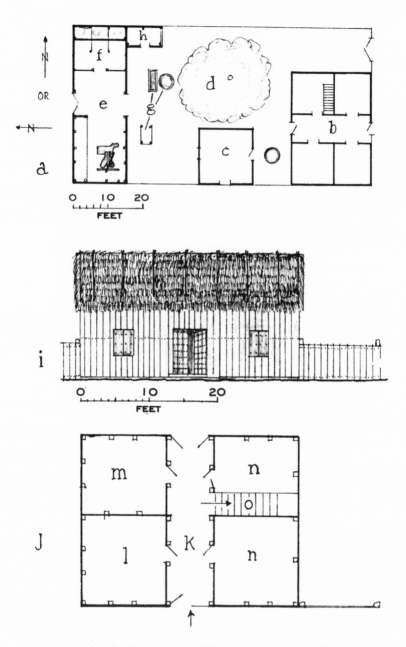

FIGURE 9.7. Plot plan for Juan Ruiz of Llerena, soldier and chief blacksmith. *A:* plot plan. *B:* house; *C:* kitchen and well; *D:* corral; *E:* smithy with forge and iron storage; *F:* stable; *G:* water trough, well, and stand for shoeing horses; *H:* chicken roost. *I:* street elevation of house. *J:* floor plan. *K:* hall; *L:* living room; *M:* dining room; *N:* bedrooms; *O:* stairs to attic. Courtesy of the St. Augustine Historical Society.

terms of man power alone, building a timberframe house cost far more than post-and-thatch or wattle-and-daub. He had to depend on coworkers such as the Basque carpenter Martín de Yztueta.

The 1590s map and other documentation make it clear that timberframe was the preferred method of construction in St. Augustine before the introduction of stonemasonry. Ruiz, as a highly skilled middle-class person, would enjoy prestige as the owner of a well-built home. His house would be similar to the delineations in figures 9.2 and 9.3 but with the simpler floor plan typical in Extremadura.

Lumber fresh from sixteenth-century sawyers was rough—far too rough to please housewives who had uncontrollable scrubbing and sweeping urges. Fortunately, the carpenter had a jack plane with a convex blade that would convert splintery surfaces into ripply ones; then he shaved the ridges off the ripples with his flooring plane, leaving a smooth, slightly textured surface that was pleasant to live with.[14]

A wide gate in the street fence gives access to both house and smithy. The house has two bedrooms, a living/dining room, and a detached kitchen. At the back of the lot the smithy has a workspace of about 15 by 18 feet (to 25 feet by 30 feet, if needed), with forge, charcoal bin, anvils, water barrel, large shears set in a tree-trunk base, plus other equipment such as a strong overhead beam (about 12 by 14 inches) and a chain to handle heavy work at the forge and anvil (figure 9.8).

I don't know whether or not Ruiz had any horses himself, but in an age of horse-drawn vehicles a blacksmith could hardly avoid fitting shoes to horses, and he needed a place to keep his four-footed customers. I put in a stable big enough for three, and just outside the smithy is the shoeing stand—a narrow U-shaped fence. The animal stands inside the U and leans against the rail while the smith does the hoof paring and shoeing.

There is also a shelter for pigs and chickens in the corral. I omitted a kitchen garden, but Ruiz might have fenced one off in the corral or somewhere else if he cared to.

He had to have help in the smithy. There must have been an apprentice or two and quite likely a "black" smith, such as one of the Crown's skilled slaves. The house has sleep space for the helpers; or they could snooze in the smithy after hours.

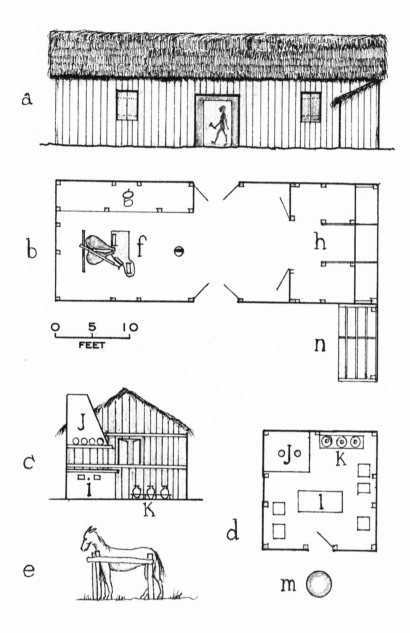

FIGURE 9.8. Smithy. *A:* smithy. *B:* floor plan of smithy and henhouse. *C:* kitchen cross section. *D:* kitchen floor plan. *E:* stand for shoeing horses. *F:* forge and anvil; *G:* iron storage; *H:* stable. *I:* stove; *J:* hood with shelf for dishes and decorations; *K:* food storage jars. *L:* table and seats; *M:* well; *N:* chicken roost. Courtesy of the St. Augustine Historical Society.

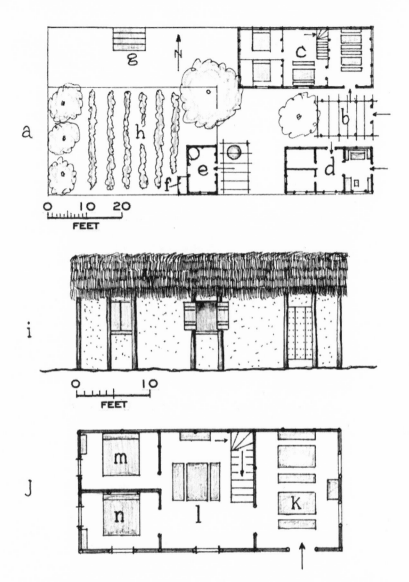

FIGURE 9.9. Plot plan for the Alonso de Olmos family, soldiers, tailors, merchants, and tav-
erners from Colomera (Andalucía). *A:* plot plan. *B:* arbor at entry gate; *C:* home for Alonso
and wife Marina, her mother Catalina, their son Antón, and Antón's Indian servant; *D:*
home for their daughter María, her lawyer husband, and their child; *E:* kitchen with stove,
oven, well, and arbor; *F:* woodshed; *G:* corral with chicken roost; *H:* kitchen garden. *I:* southern elevation of Alonso's post, wattle-and-daub house. *J:* the floor plan of Alonso's house. *K:*
tailor shop and tavern, with tables, benches, and storage chest for fabrics; *L:* living/dining
room with tables, benches, and cupboard or chest; the stairs lead to the garret bedroom for
Antón and his servant Francisco; *M:* bedroom with wardrobe for Alonso and Marina; *N:*
bedroom with wardrobe for Catalina. Courtesy of the St. Augustine Historical Society.

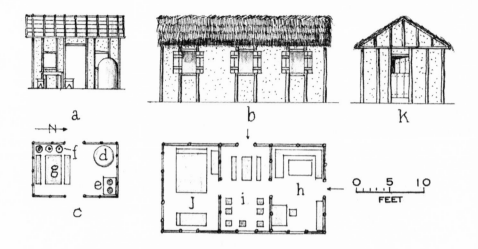

FIGURE 9.10. The Olmos kitchen and Maria's house. *A, B, and K:* the southern elevation of María's house. *C:* plan of the kitchen, which serves both families. *D:* oven; *E:* wood stove; *F:* food storage jars; *G:* table and benches. María's house, post, wattle-and-daub, also contains her husband's law office. *H:* his office, which includes writing desk with chair, bookshelf, table, and benches; *I:* the living/dining room, furnished with table, benches, chairs, and shelves; *J:* the bedroom, with wardrobe, double bed for Miguel and María, and a pallet for the children. Courtesy of the St. Augustine Historical Society.

ᔐ ᔐ ᔐ

Alonso de Olmos was a tailor. He was also a taverner and a soldier, with a four-generation family and an Indian servant who was regarded as family. Alonso, a native of Colomera, a town near Granada, came to Santa Elena in 1568, then to St. Augustine in 1576 when Santa Elena burned. His son Antón also tailored. Daughter María married a lawyer.

From the records it is obvious that Alonso crossed the ocean with the hope of improving his economic and social status and worked hard to do so. His town lot was a busy and productive place, and I have tried to place the Olmos interests in logical locations (figure 9.9). The larger of the two homes is for Grandma Catalina, Alonso, and wife Marina downstairs, and in the garret Antón and his Indian servant, Francisco. The tailor-tavern is in the same house, with two worktables, one each for the tailors and the same two for the tavern customers.

Grandmother Catalina was quite likely to be interested in gardening, raising chickens, and baking bread (which could be sold in the tavern). I have no documentation for this belief, but *my* grandmother was interested in backyard chickens and gardens.

The smaller house is for daughter María, her child, and her lawyer-husband, Miguel Delgado (figure 9.10), whose workplace has a street entry. Figure 9.10 also has the floor plan and cross section of the detached kitchen, which serves both families.[15]

RARE AMONG the hundreds of detailed reports that reached Spain from San Agustín in the early days is a description of the real estate owned by Doña María de Pomar, a property so special that it was sought, and finally bought, by the governor, Gonzalo Méndez de Canzo. This was a town lot fenced with cedar paling. (A field, location unspecified, also came with the property.) Structures on the lot included a board-and-thatch house, a small kitchen, and an arbor (*ramada*).

Although Doña María's buildings probably postdated Drake's 1586 fire, the descriptions indicate that they were in the early tradition: (1) this was upper-class property, owned by a doña and coveted for official use; (2) the site was healthful and dry, not on the waterfront; (3) the lot was fenced; (4) there was a small board-and-thatch house; (5) there was a detached board-and-thatch kitchen; (6) there was an arbor; and (7) the property included a field.

After Doña María sold these holdings to the governor, he added another room to the house, almost doubling its size. The kitchen burned; he built a larger one. Later he sold the property to the Crown for official use as the governor's residence.[1] In urging the purchase in 1604, Governor Pedro de Ybarra praised the location as a healthful one, far different from the humid waterfront house, privately owned, where two earlier governors had died and where Ybarra himself was sickly.[2]

Although the above information is known about the Pomar-Méndez de Canzo property, conjecture must serve when other "upper-class" housing is considered.

Juan Ramírez de Contreras, soldier, hunter, interpreter to Indians, was born in Baena, a town not far from Córdoba in Andalucía. He came to Florida in 1566. His expertise in the forest helped supply the garrison with meat, but his ability to palaver with the

Indians, useful as it was to the colony, eventually cost him his life. The Ais Indians of southern Florida killed him in 1597.[3]

Ramírez married María de Junco, a lady with excellent family connections. The Juncos hailed from Ribadesella, on Spain's north coast, east of Avilés. It was an area where the sunny balconies called *solanas* (*sol* means "sun") were (and are) predominant, pleasant, and useful. Surely María deserved an attractive house, and certainly Ramírez was a man who could provide one for her—with a solana included (figure 10.1).

The plot plan reflects the interests of both Ramírez and his wife. The timberframe house is about 20 by 30 feet, two-story, with balcony, kitchen, living/dining room, and bedrooms on the upper floor. Behind the house is an arbor and flower garden with a well at its center. For the hunter there is an Indian-type hut for smoking meats and a corral plus a stable (he needs the horses for his work with the Indians.)

For María, the balcony reminds her of the homeland, as do the flower garden and fruit trees. The arbor, with seats in good weather, is her outdoor living room. The chickens and the garden enrich her menus.[4]

❧ ❧ ❧

In 1567 Martín de Argüelles was mayor. A native of Pola de Siero, an inland community about 20 miles southeast of Avilés, he was one of the "Old Ones," so called because he sailed with Menéndez in 1565. He was in his early thirties then, a close associate of the adelantado—and a loyal one, as he proved again and again during the unrest and mutinies that plagued St. Augustine's early years. When he arrived he was a married man with two children, Sancho and Gerónima, and the next year his wife, Leonor de Morales, produced Martiníco, the first Spanish babe born in San Agustín. When Martiníco was ten years old, two of his uncles, Bartolomé and Juan, came to live with their brother Martín, who, by the way, owned a tavern.[5]

Housing for the Argüelles family of five or more, plus the two kinsmen, some servants, the tavern, and the mayor's political associates, must have been a problem. If Martín remembered the homes in Spain, traditional farmhouses that evolved through the centuries as efficient shelters for the people, their animals, and

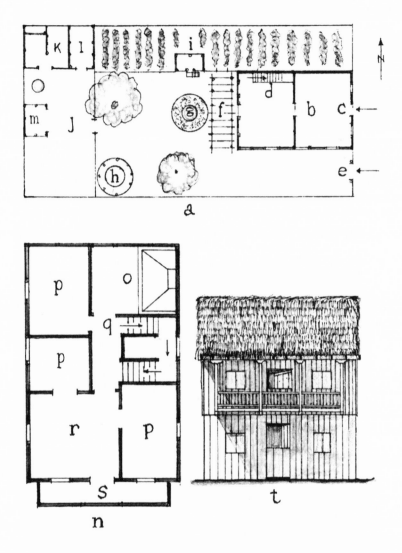

FIGURE 10.1. Plot plan for the Juan Ramírez de Contreras family. *A:* plot plan. *B:* house, ground-floor plan, containing two large storerooms; *C:* street entry; *D:* stairs to upper floor; *E:* street entry to lot; *F:* arbor; *G:* well and flower garden; *H:* hearth and smokehouse (Indian style); *I:* kitchen garden, with corn crib; *J:* corral with well; *K:* stable for horse; *L:* storage; *M:* chicken roost. *N:* second-floor plan. *O:* kitchen; *P:* bedrooms; *Q:* stairs to garret; *R:* living/dining room; *S:* balcony. *T:* street front elevation; board walling on timberframe, with thatch roof. Courtesy of the St. Augustine Historical Society.

much of their equipment and produce, then he had the problem solved. There was a balcony on the south or east face. Under the balcony, a wide entry gave access to stables on each side. In the upper story, the living room and the two bedrooms opened onto the balcony.[6] That kind of house would be comfortable in Florida, especially if those stables were bedrooms. Leonor was concerned with care and facilities for her growing family and, no doubt, with her social responsibilities as the mayor's wife, plus other duties as wife of an often absent tavern keeper. A balcony over a flower garden would be a relaxing refuge for a busy lady, and from there she would have an overview of the entire property (figure 10.3).

After Drake's fiery visit, walls of fireproof tabby must have become the preferred reconstruction material. The documents don't tell us what Argüelles built with, but I think he would prefer tabby.

Webster's defines "tabby" several ways: A mixture of lime with shell, gravel, or stones in equal proportions plus the same amount of water, forming a mass "as hard as rock" and used instead of bricks for building; a female cat; an old maid; a female gossip; silk taffeta. Setting aside the females and the taffeta, we search for Spanish definitions. *Tabíque de ostión* means a wall made of oyster shell tabby (*ostión* means large oyster). *Tapia* (from Arabic *tabiya*) means mud wall; reinforced with straw it is *tapia con paja*; plastered with lime to resist rain, it is *tapia acerada*. When you mix lime into the "mud" before you tamp it between the form boards, you have made it *tapia real*—real or royal tapia.[7]

The documents have not told us exactly when tabby was introduced into Florida. Fort construction at Santa Elena in the 1570s was described as wood, faggots (fascines), and earth "because there is neither stone nor lime or other materials." In 1577 six barrels of limestone lime were ordered from Havana to build a new fort. Then on March 25, 1580, Pedro Menéndez Marquez wrote the Crown that at Santa Elena "we have begun to make lime from oyster shells, building the houses in such manner that the Indians have lost their mettle." But by the Crown's order, Santa Elena was abandoned in 1587.[8]

So, Santa Elena lime burners moved to San Agustín. Perhaps they were recruited from San Agustín in the first place. Anyway, we can be certain that tabby was present in St. Augustine by the 1580s, particularly useful for walls.

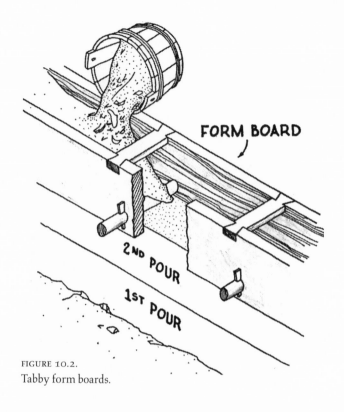

FIGURE 10.2.
Tabby form boards.

To make mud walls you need a rich, dark loam. The sandy coastal soils in the St. Augustine area did not make mud walls; they made tabby. Oyster shells were plentiful, available along the bay shores at low tide or from nearby Indian middens. The procedure was to burn the shells to make lime, the essential bonding agent. Then, using equal quantities, the soil was mixed with the lime, the shells, and the water; dumped between the form boards (figure 10.2); and packed down. It hardened after two or three days. Then the form boards were taken apart and raised to the top of the last pour. The same procedure was repeated again and again until the wall was as high as desired.

In the plot plan for Argüelles (figure 10.3), I have put his new home at the back of the lot, with four bedrooms on the ground floor and four more upstairs. The tavern, which may have been the old house, is at the front of the lot (figure 10.4). It has two rooms: the public space plus a small area for private meetings,

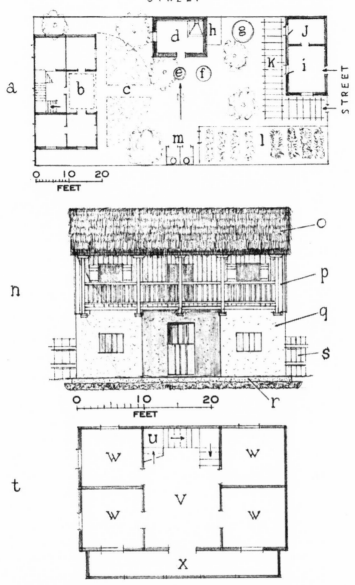

FIGURE 10.3. Plot plan for the family of Martín de Argüelles of Pola de Siero (Asturias), soldier, mayor, and taverner. *A:* plot plan. *B:* house, including a loggia; *C:* flower garden; *D:* kitchen; *E:* well; *F:* outdoor hearth; *G:* oven; *H:* woodshed; *I:* tavern; *J:* office; *K:* arbor; *L:* kitchen garden; *M:* latrine. *N:* eastern elevation. *O:* palm thatch roof; *P:* board walls, second floor; *Q:* tabby walls, ground floor; *R:* tabby foundation on oyster shell footing; *S:* board fence surrounding the lot. *T:* second floor plan; *U:* stairs to second floor; *V:* living/dining room; *W:* bedrooms; *X:* balcony. Courtesy of the St. Augustine Historical Society.

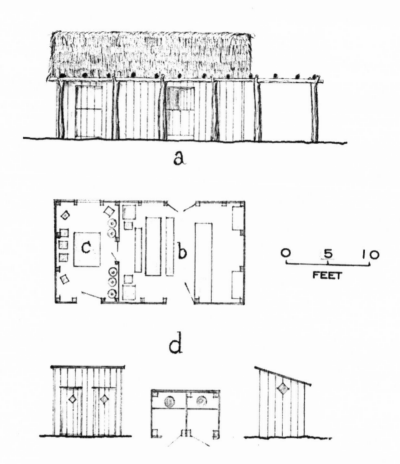

FIGURE 10.4. Argüelles tavern—board walls and thatch roof. *A:* eastern elevation with arbor. *B:* tavern floor plan, with bar, shelves, tables, benches, stools. *C:* floor plan of private office with table, chairs, and storage jars. *D:* latrine: plan, front, and side elevations; board walls and board-and-batten roof.

such as the mayor might need. Outside, a broad arbor on two sides of the building provides pleasant serving space in good weather. Taverns must have relief stations for their dedicated patrons; this one has an outdoor latrine within reach (figure 10.4).

Quarters for servants might be in the ground floor or attic of the house, or they could sleep in the tavern. There could be a kitchen in the house, but probably the best place for it is midway between the house and the tavern, where it can serve both. I have shown a kitchen with tabby walls and a tabby flat roof (figure

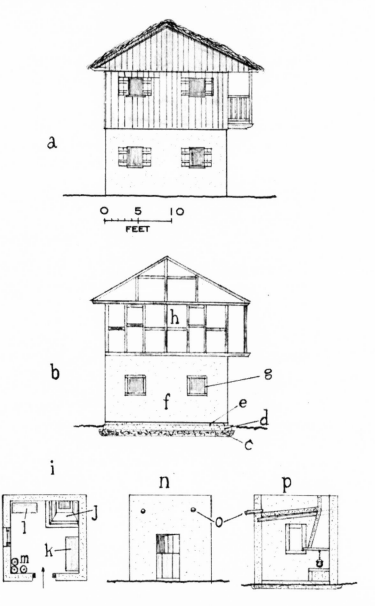

FIGURE 10.5. Argüelles house and kitchen. A: southern elevation of house. B: building materials. C: oyster shell footing; D: tabby foundation; E: tabby floor; F: exterior ground-floor
walls of tabby; G: pine door and window frames, doors, and shutters; H: pine framing for
second floor and roof; exterior walling is pine, cedar, or cypress vertical boards; palm thatch
roof. I: kitchen floor plan. J: hearth and hood; K: table; L: bench; M: food storage jars. N:
southern elevation of kitchen: foundation, walls, and flat roof are tabby. O: drain spouts. P:
kitchen section: hearth and hood are wood-framed tabby; a chain hook holds cooking pots
over the hearth fire; wooden rafters support the board ceiling on which the tabby roof is
laid; spouts drain the roof.

10.5) such as the governor reported had been built at Santa Elena. Adjacent to the kitchen are the well, the bread oven, and an outdoor hearth. A woodshed is attached to the kitchen, and there is a kitchen garden.

❧ ❧ ❧

Rodrigo de Junco signed up with Pedro Menéndez in 1562. In June 1565 his brother Juan joined the Florida expedition in Cádiz as keeper of supplies. He was twenty-six and was destined to become one of the "Old Men" of St. Augustine. Juan was transferred to Santa Elena as captain of the fort in 1576, and there he married María de Pomar.[9] They moved to St. Augustine that same year.

Juan and his wife were upper-class people who would strive for upper-class housing. I have suggested that they, like Argüelles, would want a home like they had in the homeland (figure 10.6). But in addition to the tabby and board walls, and not having tiles in Florida, I give them cypress or cedar shingles on the roof. Shingles are not fireproof, but they are less flammable than thatch.

However, Juan did use palm thatch for a hut to shelter a pair of goat herders. In the 1560s he wrote: "I made a palm hut, which cost me nothing, because the palm [leaves] used in it were brought by the Indians, and they made the hut with the help of two soldiers." Junco did admit that he gave his workers about eight pounds of bread and "a little" wine.[10]

❧ ❧ ❧

Pedro Menéndez Marquez, the nephew of Pedro Menéndez de Avilés, served him as sea captain, accountant, and collector of the Mexican subsidy and was himself governor of Florida from 1577 until his resignation in 1594 due to illness. Doña María de Solís was his wife.[11] This Don Pedro has been called "the last of the Asturian Dynasty," and he certainly deserves recognition. For that reason I suggest that he had a roomy house of Asturian plan, with the family coat of arms on the front façade (figures 10.7 and 10.8). Such memorials can be seen on ancient homes in Spain today.

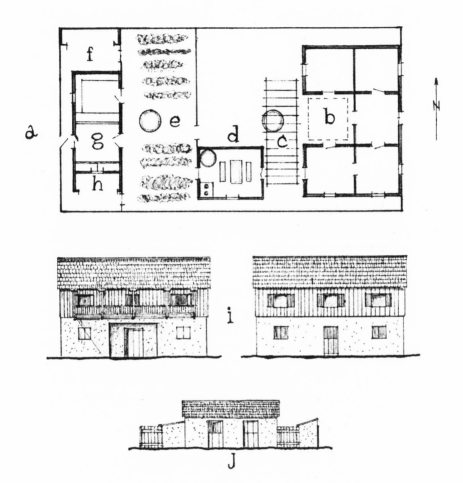

FIGURE 10.6. Plot plan for captain and factor Juan de Junco, from Ribadesella (Asturias). *A:*
plot plan: the lot is fenced with boards. *B:* house: tabby walls on ground floor; rooms include
office (at the street entrance), living room, dining room, bedrooms, and loggia; *C:* arbor and
well; *D:* kitchen, with stove, oven, table, and benches; *E:* kitchen garden and well; *F:* pigsty;
G: stable and storage; *H:* chicken roost. *I:* house elevations: western (left) and eastern (right);
the upper floor (bedrooms) is timberframe with board walls and shingle roof. *J:* eastern
elevation of stable with chicken roost (left) and pigsty (right). Courtesy of the St. Augustine Historical Society.

STREET

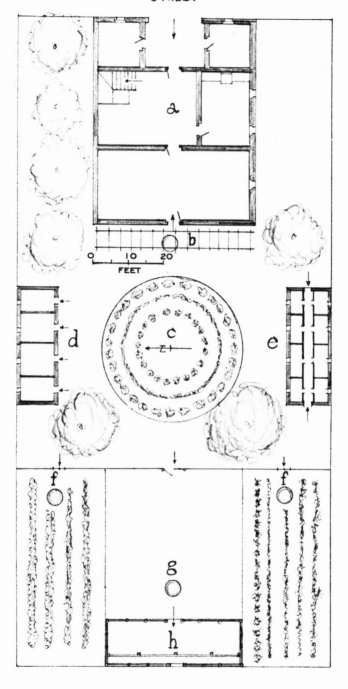

a

0   10   20
FEET

b

c

d

e

f

f

g

h

FIGURE 10.7. *(facing page)* Plot plan for the governor. The governor's town lot was probably a *caballería* (knight-size, 88 x 176 U.S. feet) instead of the usual *peonía* (44 x 88 feet) of ordinary folk. *A:* house for the governor, his wife, and their two children. *B:* arbor and well. *C:* flower garden. *D:* quarters for Catalina (the governor's widowed sister), fort chaplain Alonso Cabezas, Capt. Francisco Salazar and wife, and Ens. Pedro Menéndez de Avilés. *E:* servants' quarters. *F:* kitchen gardens and wells. *G:* corral and well. *H:* stable. Courtesy of the St. Augustine Historical Society.

FIGURE 10.8. Menéndez coat of arms. The device of the ship breaking the chain between two castles (on a red field) was granted to Ruy Pérez de Avilés, a paternal ancestor who in 1248 armed his vessels with iron-toothed prows and severed the Moorish chain defending the river at Sevilla. Ravens paired on a silver field signify the Arango family of Don Pedro's mother. Courtesy of the St. Augustine Historical Society.

I also have shown a "bathroom" (figure 10.9j) on the second floor, mainly because I remember one in the Asturian Palacio de Nubledo, which I recorded in 1962. Deposits in the Palacio's upper-story "bathroom" simply dropped to the ground below, to be carried off to the dung heap, whereas this bathroom (figure 10.9j), because it has no overhang, must have a container to be removed and cleaned daily.[12]

Upper-class people had responsibilities. For instance, this governor provided quarters not only for kinfolk, servants, chaplain, and Capt. Francisco Salazar and his wife, but he brought in two young Indian girls, future chieftainesses, to be raised in his house and to attend Doña María. He needed a caballería-size lot to provide all the living quarters required (figure 10.9).[13]

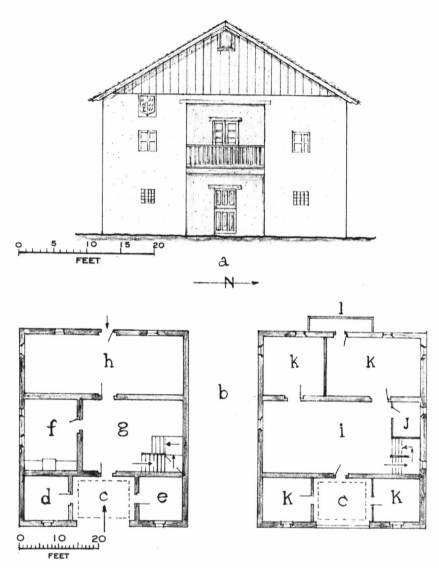

FIGURE 10.9. Home of Gov. Pedro Menéndez Marquez. *A:* eastern elevation. The walls are tabby (lime, sand, and oyster shell aggregate plus lime plaster). Cedar shingles cover the roof; vertical boards seal the gables, except for a small vent at the peak. The family coat of arms is displayed on the street facade (upper left). *B:* floor plans: ground floor (left) and upper floor (right). *C:* loggias; *D:* guardroom; *E:* governor's office; *F:* kitchen; *G:* dining room with stairs to upper floor; *H:* meeting room; *I:* living room with stairs to garret; *J:* bathroom; *K:* bedrooms; *L:* balcony. Courtesy of the St. Augustine Historical Society.

Epilogue

THE NATURE OF the housing and organization of space used by colonists in a new and strange environment was influenced both by the familiar traditions of their native provinces and by the demands of the new settings. The work of a transplanted craftsman, although rooted in a homeland tradition, was bound to reflect the demands and resources of his new surroundings as well as his observation and acceptance of unfamiliar practices.

Spain's vernacular architecture evolved through the centuries to meet specific needs. The faint traces of sixteenth-century Spanish structures uncovered archaeologically in Florida, even when illuminated with information from written records, fail to give a definitive picture of St. Augustine's physical appearance. In the absence of that picture, I looked to the architectural manifestations in the Americas. Specifically, because Florida had no monumental buildings, I looked to the vernacular or "folk" architecture. Analyses of the vernacular constructions, many of which evolved long before Columbus set sail, helped to interpret cryptic evidence from the ground or in the documents. Used with logic and care, this study has suggested suitable replacements for missing structural elements and details.

The nature of houses themselves depended upon the social standing and occupation of the inhabitants. Three levels of European society were present in sixteenth-century St. Augustine. One was comprised of an upper class of people who did not work with their hands, such as royal officials or others who had profitable connections with the leadership. Members of the second level, the middle class, often worked with their hands, but as skilled persons (master craftsmen, merchants). This group had useful trades, professions, or opportunities connected with the leadership. Members of the lower class all worked with their hands. They made up the majority of St. Augustine's population, comprised of common soldiers and settlers with few resources.

Factors such as the three-level society of St. Augustine further refined available documentary and cartographic sources and the historical deductions based on them. These deductions and interpretations, when combined with the physical evidence of archaeology from sixteenth-century sites in St. Augustine, permit a reliable reconstruction of the community.

Timberframe Techniques in Spain

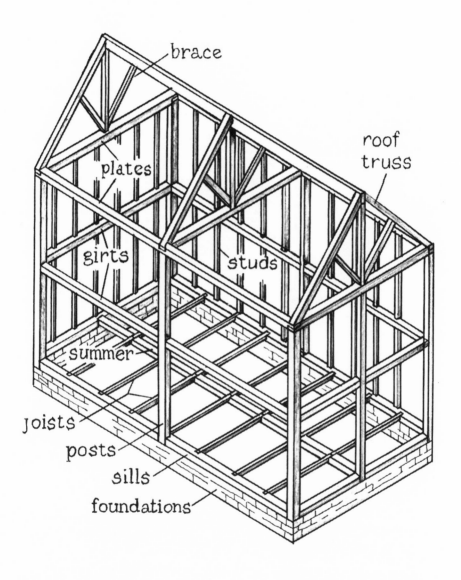

FIGURE A.1. Mainframe nomenclature. Courtesy of the St. Augustine Historical Society.

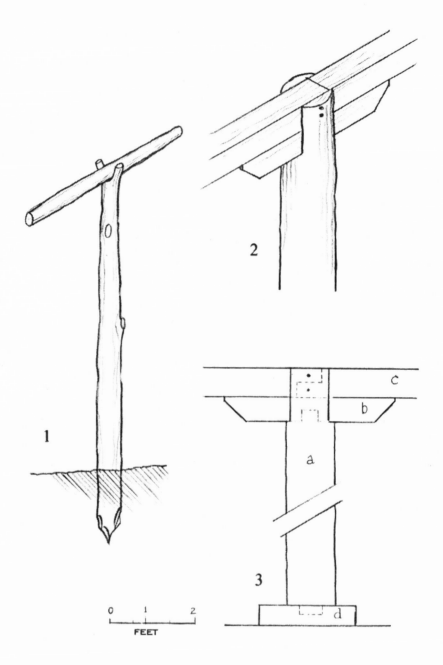

FIGURE A.2. Support posts. *1:* post for supporting an arbor. *2:* post notched at the top to receive beam supports and beams. *3* shows *A:* post; *B:* beam support; *C:* beams; *D:* anchor for the post.

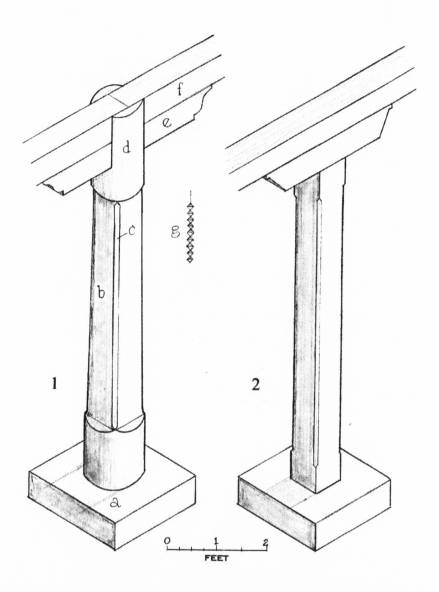

FIGURE A.3. Types of decorative support posts. Posts 1 and 2: *A:* anchor for the post; *B:* post squared; *C:* post flatted. *D:* the top of the post remains round, as does the base; the top receives *E:* the beam support and *F:* the beam. *G:* the small rectangles represent the notches sometimes used to decorate the corners of square posts.

TIMBERFRAME TECHNIQUES IN SPAIN

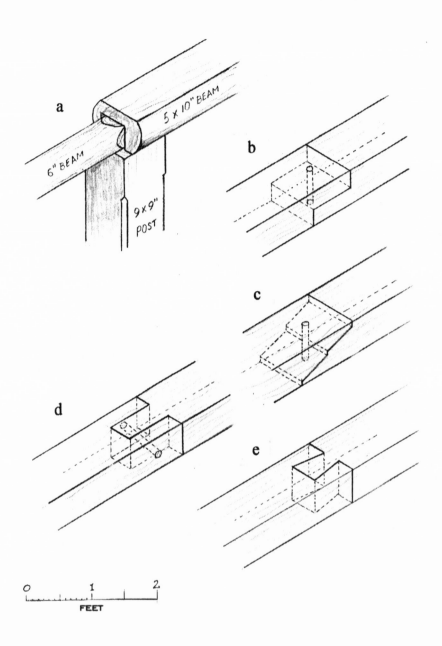

FIGURE A.4. Beam splices. *A:* 5 x 10 inch beam ends on the 9 x 9 inch post. The 6-inch beam nestles into the end of the 5 x 10 inch beam. A spike through the beams into the top of the post will anchor them. The four other illustrations (*B–E*) show various splices that are seated atop the posts. Three of the splices (*B–D*) are held together by wooden or iron rods, but the tongue of *E* is an anchor.

128   APPENDIX

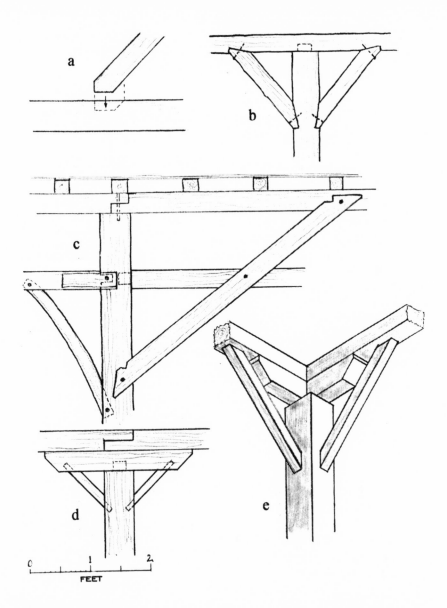

FIGURE A.5. Post-and-beam splices. *A:* a brace being set into the overhead beam of a door-way; the upper end of the brace will be set into a vertical king post, which reaches to the roof plate. *B:* post and beam, with two braces. *C:* post and four beams; the post has two lower beams about a foot below the upper beams, which carry floor rafters; two braces are also on the post: the short one at left braces the left, whereas the long one on the right touches not only the post but the low beam and the high beam. *D:* post and beam support, with anchors and beam junction above. *E:* post with the right-angled beam support and beam above.

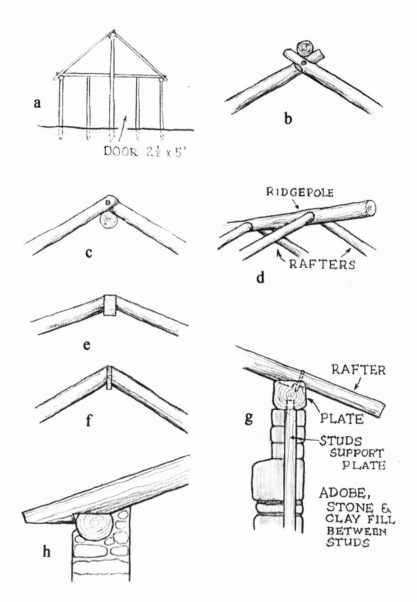

FIGURE A.6. Rafter splices. *A:* sketch of framework at entry of the structure. *B:* rafters joined at roof peak with ridgepole above. *C:* rafters joined at roof peak with ridgepole below. *D:* rafters joined at roof peak with rafter ends joined into the ridgepole. *E:* rafters joined at roof peak with rafter ends joined to squared ridgeplate. *F:* rafters joined at roof peak with rafter ends joined to flatted ridgeplate. *G:* studs support the plates, which anchor the rafters; the space between the wooden studs was filled with earth, wood, stone, and other materials. *H:* stone-walled houses often supported lumber that served as ridgepoles; it was flatted on top to anchor the foot of the ridgepole.

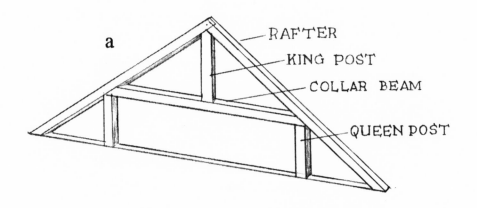

a

RAFTER

KING POST

COLLAR BEAM

QUEEN POST

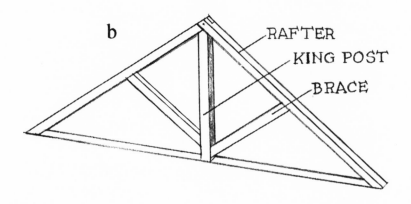

b

RAFTER

KING POST

BRACE

FIGURE A.7. Rafter supports. *A:* rafters on tie beam, with collar beam, king post, and queen post. *B:* rafters on tie beam with king post and braces.

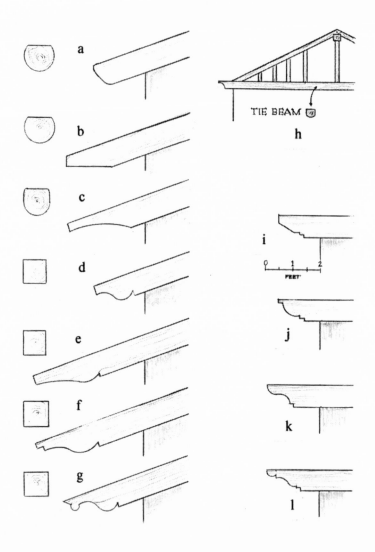

FIGURE A.8. Decorative treatments of eave ends. *A–G:* rafter eave ends. *H:* mainframe. *I–L:* tie beams with decorative ends.

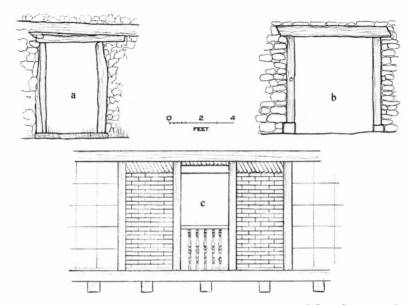

FIGURE A.9. Ground-floor and upper-floor doorways. *A–B:* ground-floor doorways. *C:* upper-floor doorway.

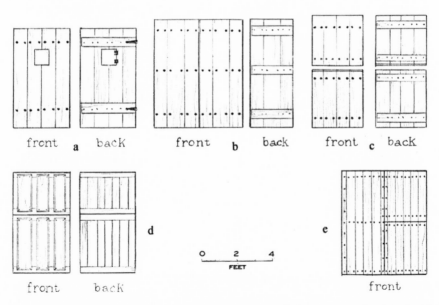

FIGURE A.10. Door types. *A:* front and back doors with small shutters at eye level. *B:* double front doors with back showing construction. *C:* double (up and down) door with back view showing construction. *D:* double (up and down) door with panels. *E:* double door with the right half shown in two sections.

TIMBERFRAME TECHNIQUES IN SPAIN

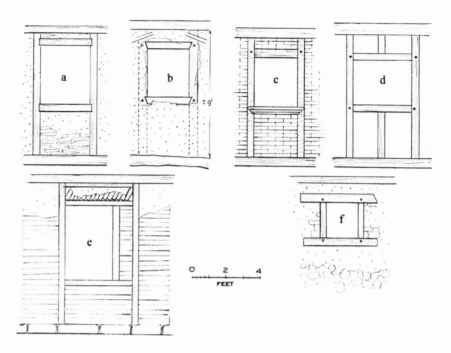

FIGURE A.11. Window types. *A:* window frame anchored between upper and lower beams; horizontal members are notched into the vertical beams. *B:* frame partly obscured by the plaster that covers the exterior walls. *C:* window frame in a brick wall; the vertical beams extend to the structural beams above and below, but they are covered with plaster; the sill of this opening, however, projects conspicuously from the frame. *D:* empty frame. *E:* window frame in a brick wall; it has lost most of the plaster that covered it. *F:* small opening to ventilate a ground-floor room.

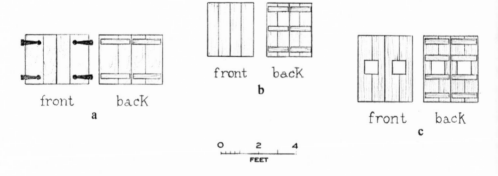

FIGURE A.12. Shutter types. *A:* two-leaf, board and batten; opens out. *B:* two-leaf, board and batten (variant); opens out. *C:* two-leaf, board and batten with apertures; opens in.

Notes

Chapter 1: Archaeological Background

1. Smith, *Before the White Man*, 30.

2. Gordon, *Report on the 1992 Excavations at the Fountain of Youth Park*, 51–52; and introduction by Kathleen Deagan, "Summary Interpretation of 1991 Archaeological Field Work at the Fountain of Youth Park Site," 19–22.

3. Deagan, *Archaeological Strategy*, 2ff., 80–87, 92, 110, 122–23, 132–35. See also Fernández-Sardina, *Archaeological Investigations at the Ximénez-Fatio Annex*, 2, 17, 29–32. His finds included a "sleeper log" footer, postmolds, and lime-reducing pits.

4. Chaney, *Report on the 1985 Excavations at the Fountain of Youth Site*, 97; Smith, *Before the White Man*, 17, 20; Feagin, "'Diggers' Hope to Find Menendez Colony Site," 1.

Chapter 2: How It Began

1. Morison, *Admiral of the Ocean Sea*, 82, 85–88, 96–103, 106–7, 660–67; Weber, *Spanish Frontier in North America*, 20–25; Wells, *Outline of History*, 780, 783, 786; Wilgus and D'Eca, *Latin American History*, 22–23, 29–20.

2. Bennett, *Settlement of Florida*, 94–95; Lyon, *Enterprise of Florida*, 37–41.

3. Manucy, *Florida's Menéndez*, 27.

Chapter 3: Early Days

1. Manucy, *Florida's Menéndez*, 27–33.

2. Gannon, *Cross in the Sand*, 26–27, citing the account of Fr. Francisco López de Mendoza Grajales.

3. Chatelain, *Defenses*, 41; Mendoza, "Relación," in Ruidíaz, *La Florida* 2:431–65; Gannon, *Cross in the Sand*, 26; Manucy, *Florida's Menéndez*.

4. Manucy, *Florida's Menéndez*, 35–47; Manucy, "The Man Who Was Menéndez."

5. Bushnell, *King's Coffer*, frontispiece.

6. Bennett, *Settlement of Florida*, Le Moyne's drawings.

7. Lyon, *Forts Caroline and San Mateo*, 10, 30ff.

8. Bushnell, *King's Coffer*, 8.

9. Lyon, "Cultural Brokers in 16th Century Florida," 0–5; Lyon, *Enterprise of Florida*, 14–18.

10. Deagan, "1580 Timucua," 103.

11. Manucy, Fieldbook IV, 4.

12. Deagan, "1580 Timucua," 103.

13. Manucy, "Recommendations for Timucua Structures," 23, 32.

14. Manucy, "Building Materials in 16th Century St. Augustine."

15. Manucy, *Houses,* 63A, from photo, courtesy of R. H. Stewart, National Geographic Society.

16. Manucy, Fieldbook VI, 4; Flores, *Arquitectura* 3:527.

17. Deagan, "1580 Timucua," 56, 98–99, 103.

18. Manucy, Fieldbook VI, 9–10.

19. Bennett, *Settlement of Florida*, 50–51.

CHAPTER 4: AN UNSETTLED SETTLEMENT

1. Barrientos, *Pedro Menéndez de Avilés*, 106–7. San Mateo (St. Matthew) was the name given French Fort Caroline after its capture by the Spanish.

2. Connor, "Wooden Forts," 104–6.

3. Lucuze, *Principios*, 61–62.

4. Connor, "Wooden Forts," 106; Connor, *Colonial Records* 2:3–7.

5. Alonso de las Alas to Philip III, January 12, 1600, cited in Connor, "Wooden Forts," 109.

6. Solís de Merás, *Pedro Menéndez*, 200–10; Chatelain, *Defenses*, 42–43, 136n. 1.

7. Connor, "Wooden Forts," 107; Hoffman, "Project for Reconstruction," 1–2.

8. Connor, "Wooden Forts," 109–10.

9. Bushnell, "Noble and Loyal City," 36.

10. Walter Bigges, *A Summarie and True Discourse of Sir Francis Drake's West Indies Voyage* (London, 1589), cited in Connor, "Wooden Forts," 110–11.

11. "Memorial, letters and plans, Hernando de Mestas, Feb., 1595," cited in Connor, "Wooden Forts," 171–72.

12. Ibid.

13. Chatelain, *Defenses*, 54, 56.

CHAPTER 5: TWO ACCOUNTS, TWO MAPS

1. Lowery, *Catalogue*, 2:693–712, from Dirección de Hidrografía, Madrid, Colección Navarrete, T 14 E No. 47.

2. Velázquez, *Dictionary*; Brockman, *Trees of North America*.

3. Testimony of Juan de Junco, December 10, 1569, et. seq., and others in the *residencia* taken by Castillo y Ahedo, 1576; *AGI, EC* 154-A, fols. 1203v, 1206v, 1212, 1228v, 1240, 1320.

4. Historian Paul Hoffman found the name of San Agustín's parish church in the Archivo Histórico Nacional, Ordenas Militares, Expediente 5213, Declaración de Doña Mayor de Arango, Avilés, October 1611; Chatelain, *Defenses,* maps 2 and 4.

5. Narrative of Andrés de San Miguel, in García, *Relaciones,* 156ff.

6. García, *Relaciones,* 195.

7. Ibid., 196.

8. Ibid., 205–6.

9. Ibid., 201.

10. Ibid., 206–7.

11. Ibid., 206.

12. Ibid., 202.

13. Connor, "Wooden Forts," 171, citing Pedro Menéndez Marquez to the Crown, December 27, 1583; Connor, *Colonial Records* 2:282–83, citing Pedro Menéndez Marquez to the Crown, March 25, 1580.

CHAPTER 6: MATERIALS THAT BUILT THE TOWN

1. Soil Conservation Service, *Soil Survey,* 93; Deagan, *Archaeological Strategy,* 51–58; *AGI EC* 154A, fols. 551v–59.

2. Chatelain, *Defenses,* 54–56; Florida Division of Forestry, *Forest Trees,* 3–4, 10, 12; Brockman, *Trees of North America,* 2, 8, 32, 52–53, 64–65.

3. Hoffman and Lyon, "Factors' Accounts, 1591–1594."

4. Connor, "Wooden Forts," 110.

5. Connor, *Colonial Records* 2:154.

6. Ibid.; Manucy, Measured Drawings Notebook, 34, 37, 49, 50, and Fieldbook IV, 34; Velázquez, *Dictionary;* Wilson, "Gulf Coast Architecture," 80.

7. Connor, *Colonial Records* 2:126, 128, Declaration of Gonzáles and Martín, August 20, 1608, *AGI, SD* 232.

8. Florida Division of Forestry, *Forest Trees,* 16.

9. Manucy, *Houses,* 99–102; de Rojas, *Protocolos de la Habana* 1:38, Protocolo de Pérez de Barrato; Cuyas and Llana, *English-Spanish Dictionary; Jacksonville (FL) Tourguide Map,* 1974; Soil Conservation Service, *Soil Survey.*

10. Connor, *Colonial Records* 2:190.

11. Méndez de Canzo, Papers relating to the sale of Governor Méndez de Canzo's house, *AGI, SD* 82, 1603–4; Méndez de Canzo, Ybarra to the Crown, February 10, 1605, *AGI, SD* 224.

12. Connor, *Colonial Records* 2:126, 282–85; Sánchez de Mercado, March 1580, cited in Vigneras, "Fortificaciónes de la Florida," 543; Accounts of Juan Menéndez Marquez, June 27, 1592, payment to Juan Sánchez, lime burner, for 46 pipes of lime to make an *azotea* for the accountant's quarters and magazines, *AGI, CD* 949.

13. Connor, *Colonial Records* 2:272–73; Accounts of Juan Menéndez

Marquez: payment to Juan Sánchez, June 27, 1592, *AGI, CD;* Vigneras, "Fortificaciónes," 543.

14. Deagan, *Archaeological Strategy,* 51–58; Soil Conservation Service, *Soil Survey,* 93.

15. Governor Ybarra to Crown, July 31, 1608, *AGI, SD* 224, *SC.* For details on tabby construction, see Manucy, "Tapia or Tabby," 32–33.

16. Manucy, Measured Drawings Notebook, 50, 58.

17. Deagan, *Archaeological Strategy,* 42–50.

18. Declaration of Gonzáles and Martín, August 20, 1608, *AGI, SD* 232; Connor, *Colonial Records* 2:250–51; Treasury accounts for Spanish Florida, cited in Hoffman, "A Study of Defense Costs, 1565–1585."

CHAPTER 7: PEOPLE, PLANS, SHELTERS

1. Aguilera, "Provisional Report on the Ethnohistory"; Manucy, "Toward Re-Creation of 16th Century St. Augustine," 3.

2. Deagan, *Archaeological Strategy,* 87; Deagan, "St. Augustine: First Urban Enclave," 190, 198–99; Hoffman and Lyon, "Layout of St. Augustine, Florida, c. 1580"; Manucy, "The Town Plan."

3. Menéndez, *AGI, J* 999, no. 2, ramo 9 (September 1566).

4. Hoffman, "Inventories of Personal Property," 11 and 14, *AGI, EC* 154A, fols. 782–783v, 791v–792.

5. Deagan, *Archaeological Strategy,* 87.

6. I Kings 21:21.

7. Deuteronomy 23:9–14.

8. Loriga, "Seccion de Humor," 196.

9. Lyon, Letter to Rolleston and Manucy, August 15, 1978, citing the Escobedo poem in Biblioteca Nacional MS 187, fol. 330; Bennett, *Settlement,* 63.

10. See figure 5.7.

11. Manucy, Fieldbook VII, 116–17; photos 3–61 (1973–74 series) 2/21.

12. Apple, *The Hawaiian Thatched House,* 89, 133–35.

13. See figures 3.12, 7.8, and 7.9, which illustrate thatching techniques. For more details, see Manucy, "Timucua Structures," 32ff.

14. *America's Fascinating Indian Heritage,* 95; Deagan, "1580 Timucua," 56 (citing Challeaux), 64.

CHAPTER 8: HUMBLE HOMES

1. Hoffman and Lyon, "Information on St. Augustine Personnel c. 1580 from Study of the Garrison Musters," 2. Hereafter cited as "Garrison Musters."

2. Deagan, "1580 Timucua," 45, 57, 68–69, 103–5.

3. Hoffman and Lyon, "Garrison Musters," 6; Aguilera, "Provisional Report," 8; Manucy, "Timucua Structures."

4. Peterson, Charles E., "Houses of French St. Louis," 17–40 plus illustrations, in *Building Early America*.

5. *Webster's Dictionary*.

6. Flores, *Arquitectura* 2:173.

7. Dirreción General de Arquitectura.

8. Manucy, Fieldbook I, 7–8.

9. Flores, *Arquitectura* 2:172, 284–85; 3:346, 350–51.

10. Flores, *Arquitectura* 3:350–51, figures 465–67; 346 figure 456.

11. Flores, *Arquitectura* 2:172, 243, 275, 278–79, 284–85; 3:346, 350 figure 465.

12. Deagan, *Archaeological Strategy*, 76; Deagan, "Spanish St. Augustine: America's First Melting Pot," 22–30.

13. Soil Conservation Service, *Soil Survey*, 6.

14. *AGI, EC* 154A, 551–59.

15. *St. Augustine Record*, "Sands of Time," June 10, 1935, 8, 10–11.

16. Soil Conservation Service, *Soil Survey*, 6, 93, 113, 118, and map 29.

17. Deagan, *Archaeological Strategy*, 76; Deagan, "America's First Melting Pot," 22–30; personal communications.

18. Hoffman and Lyon, "Garrison Musters," 4.

19. Hoffman, "Garrison List, 1578."

20. Manucy, Fieldbook II, 50–52.

21. Hoffman, "List of Characters," 4.

Chapter 9: Middle-Class Homes

1. Manucy, *Menéndez*, 38–39; Hoffman, "Garrison List, 1578."

2. Flores, *Arquitectura* 2:66, figures 74, 75, 77, 78. These are sketches of the framing for early *caseríos*. Figure 74 is from Caro Baroja and records the façade of "the most archaic type" of *caserío* in Guipúzcoa Province. The other figures are caseríos of Ataún (Guipúzcoa). J. Arin Dorronsoro sketched the framing of these structures, showing the placement of posts, studs, laterals, braces and also beams tying together the tops of the posts in each corridor. Dorronsoro dates his figure 75 structure about 1600. Ataún is only a couple of miles south of Yztueta's hometown of Lazcano. Caro Baroja, *Vasconiana*; also his *Los Vascos*.

3. Manucy, *Houses*, 17, 19–20.

4. Bealer, *Old Ways of Working Wood*, 49–50.

5. Armada Real Accounts, 1576, *AGI, CD* 513.

6. Kelly, *Domestic Architecture of Connecticut*, 41; de Rojas, *Indice y Extractos del Archivo de Protocolos*, 1578–87, 1:38, Protocolo de Juan Pérez de Borrotol.

7. Manucy, Measured Drawings Notebooks, no. 1, H1-H7.

8. Peterson, *The Rules of Work of the Carpenters Company*, plate V.

9. Rebolledo, *Construcción General*, plate 4, figure 99; plate 6, figure 100.

10. Bealer, *Old Ways of Working Wood*, 52, 88–90, 110–15.

11. *AGI, EC* 1024A, fols. 23–24; Accounts of Juan de Junco, Factor, *AGI, CD* 941; Deagan, *Archaeological Strategy*, 124–25, 127; Lyon, "Typology of Nails," 1–3, citing *AGI*, Mapas y Planos, Ingenios Y Maestres, 34; *AGI, CD* 462, no. 9 (1578); Declaration of Gonzáles and Martín, August 20, 1608, *AGI, SD* 232.

12. Hoffman, "Garrison List, 1578"; Hoffman, "List of Characters."

13. Flores, *Arquitectura* 3:492, figure 696; Manucy, Fieldbook VI, 23, 26.

14. Bealer, *Old Ways of Working Wood*, 168.

15. Hoffman, Lyon, Manucy and Rolleston, "Personnel Reservoir," 13, 15, 32, 33; *AGI, CD* 941; *AGI, EC* 154A, fols. 467–505; Hoffman and Lyon, "Garrison Musters," 2.

Chapter 10: Upper-Class Homes

1. Papers relating to the sale of Governor Méndez de Canzo's St. Augustine house, 1603–4, *AGI, SD* 82.

2. Ybarra to the Crown, January 8, 1604, *AGI, SD* 224.

3. Testimonio de la ynformación que se hizo sobre la muerte de Juan Ramírez de Contreras, November 30–December 1, 1597, *AGI* 54-5-16.

4. For descriptions of folk architecture on the north coast, see Flores, *Arquitectura* 2:160–72; for photos and scale drawings of *solanas* in Avilés, see Manucy, Measured Drawings Notebook 1, 46–56; for photos 3–61 see Manucy, Photographs, 1962–63 series, 115, 116.

5. Menéndez, Lista de la gente de Guerra . . . , *AGI, EC* 154A, fol. 1279v; *National Geographic Magazine*, Spain and Portugal, Atlas Plate 33; Lyon, *Enterprise*, 151; DeCoste, *First Child of Spanish Florida*, 2–3, 6.

6. Hoyos, *La Casa Tradicional en España*, 7; Manucy, Fieldbook I, 54, home of Manuel Yuste; photos 3–61 (1962–63 series) 137 and 138; Manucy, Measured Drawings Notebook 1, 51–56, house of Menéndez Suárez; photos 3–61 (1962–63 series) 107, 108, and 128.

7. Velázquez, *Dictionary*.

8. Connor, *Colonial Records* 2:282–83; Lyon, *Santa Elena: A Brief History*, 15; South, *Testing Archaeological Sampling Methods*, 22.

9. Bushnell, *Coffer*, 54, 121, 143–45; Hoffman, "Garrison List, 1578"; 1; Lyon, *Enterprise*, 74n. 9, 75, 88, 151, 160, 164, 167.

10. Lyon, "Analysis of the 'Livestock-Fish-Banquet-Game' Case," citing *AGI, EC* 154A, fol. 1203v.

11. Bushnell, *Coffer*, 17 and appendixes 1 and 2; Manucy, Fieldbook 7, "Menéndez Marquez Genealogy."

12. Manucy, Measured Drawings Notebook H-1, 58; H-2, 18; H-3, 7.

13. Manucy, Fieldbook 7, "Menéndez Marquez Genealogy."

Glossary

Adobe. Sun-dried clay.

Arbor. Latticework frame covered with vines or other plants for shade.

Arroba. Spanish weight of 25 pounds; a measure containing about 4 gallons.

Auger. A tool for boring holes. Archaeologists use it to obtain earth samples.

Azotea. Flat slab roof.

Balcony. Platform projecting from the wall of a building, supported by brackets and enclosed by a balustrade.

Batten. Strip of wood used to cover the joints between boards.

Bay. Principal part of a structure.

Biscocho. Hardtack.

Breastwork. A defensive work of moderate height, hastily thrown up.

Broadaxe. Axe with a broad blade for cutting timber and flatting its surfaces.

Caballería. Town lot land grant of 100 by 200 Spanish feet (88 by 176 U.S. feet) to upper class, plus additional lands for farming and grazing.

Cadalecho. Continuous bunk, made of tree branches, along the inner walls of Indian lodges.

Cal. Lime; lime mortar, plaster, tabby. Florida lime was calcined from shells, usually oyster shells from Indian middens.

Casa. House.

Caserío. Basque farmhouse.

Cavalier. A defense elevation of earth, bordered with a parapet.

Century plant. A tropical American agave, having fleshy leaves and a tall stalk with greenish flowers; so named because it was mistakenly thought to bloom only once a century.

Choir Loft. Gallery occupied by the church choir.

Cob. Unburned clay mixed with straw and used as wall material.

Corral. A fenced yard.

Curtains. Exterior fort walls.

Daub. Clay used on wattle walls as plaster.

Encina. Oak tree.

Eave. The edge of a roof.

Esparto grass. A long, coarse grass of southern Spain, used to make paper, cordage, shoes, baskets, etc.

Eucalyptus. A genus of subtropical evergreen trees of the myrtle family.

Façade. Exterior face of a building.

Faggot. Bundle of sticks used for various purposes in fortification.

Fascine. Bundle of sticks used in raising parapets in fortification.

Gable. The triangular wall enclosed by the ends of the house roof.

Garret. Room just below the house roof; attic.

Guano. Palm thatch; bird droppings.

Harina. Flour.

Hearth. The floor of a fireplace.

Jacal. Indian lodge.

Joist. Any of the parallel timbers that support a floor or ceiling.

King post. Vertical beam in the roof frame, between the horizontal tie beam and the roof ridge.

Lath. One of the wood strips which are the bed for plaster.

Lintel. The headpiece of wood or stone over a door, window, or other opening, to support the weight above.

Loggia. A gallery or arcade open to the air on at least one side; especially one contained within the body of a building and serving as an open-air room.

Midden. Refuse heap, marking the site of primitive habitation.

Molding. Any of various ornamental contours given to cornices, jambs, etc.; a shaped wood strip used as an ornament.

Nombre de Dios. Name of God; the mission at Seloy village.

Ostión. Large oyster.

Pale. Fence.

Palisade. A fence of stakes for defense.

Palma. Palm tree; palm thatch.

Parapet. Breast-high wall to screen troops from frontal fire.

Patio. Courtyard; or inner area of the yard open to the sky.

Peonía. Town lot given to a settler; 50 by 100 Spanish feet (44 ft by 88 ft U.S.), plus additional lands for farming and grazing.

Pie. One foot, Spanish measure (11 inches U.S.).

Pinos. Pines.

Pinos gruesos. Large pines.

Pipas. Iron-hooped barrels.

Plate. A horizontal girder that supports vertical timbers.

Plaza. Open square or marketplace, in town for public use.

Pole. A long, slender piece of wood.

Postmold. Evidence in the ground of a post that has rotted away.

Purlin. Horizontal timber supporting common rafters.

Queen post. Either of two vertical posts between tie beam and rafter.

Rafter. Timber that extends from eave to roof ridge to support the roof cover.

Ramada. Arbor.

Ridgeplate. Horizontal support for rafters at the roof peak; ridgepole.

Ridgepole. See Ridgeplate.

Roble. Oak tree.

Roof plate. Horizontal timber atop the house walls, upon which rafters are seated.

Roof post. Vertical support for the ridgepole.

Row houses. Houses which front on the street with no space between them.

Sabina, savino, savina. Red cedar (*Juniperus silicicola*) posts used for house wall construction and for shingles. Both cypress and cedar were preferred as rot resistant.

Sala. Hall; living room.

Solana. Open porch or gallery for "taking the sun"; an elevated porch.

Tabby. Mixture of lime, oyster shells, sand, and water to make walls, roofs, and floors.

Tabíque de ostión. Wall made of oyster shell tabby.

Tabla. Board.

Tablón. Plank (larger than board).

Tapia. Mud wall; measure of a mud wall containing 50 square feet.

Tapia acerada. Lime-plastered mud wall.

Tapia con paja. Mud wall with straw.

Tapia real. Wall made of rammed earth and lime.

Tapial. Mold for making mud walls.

Tasajo. Dried beef.

Tejamaniles. Shingles.

Terreplein. The top deck of a fort, behind the parapets.

Thatch. Roofing material of palm leaves, straw, etc.

Tie beam. A beam serving as a tie.

Timberframe. Framework of wood.

Trenail. Wooden peg used to join timbers.

Trestle. A horizontal beam fastened to two pairs of spread legs. Two such trestles can support a tree trunk to be sawn into boards.

Wattle. Woven work made of sticks intertwined with twigs or branches, used for walls, fences, and roofs.

Wattle-and-daub. A wattled network of twigs daubed over with clay and mud.

Whitewash. Lime in water for painting wood or masonry surfaces to improve weather resistance and appearance.

Wythe. Flexible branch or twig used in wattle construction.

Zapata. A short horizontal member on the head of a vertical post.

Bibliography

Archival Sources

ARCHIVO DE PROTOCOLOS DE SEVILLA

Books of 1580, Oficio XIX, fol. 1011.

ARCHIVO DEL INSTITUTO DE DON JUAN, MADRID

Envío 25, H, No. 162.

ARCHIVO GENERAL DE INDIAS, SEVILLE

Audiencia de Santo Domingo. Legajo 82, 116, 125, 224, 229, 231–32, 2528, 2595. Cited as SD in the notes.
Casa de Contratación. Legajo 58, 204, 2932, 3908–9.
Contaduría General. Legajo 301, 312, 462, 513, 941–44, 948–49. Cited as CD in the notes.
Escribanía de Cámara. Legajo 23–24, 34v–43v, 154A–55, 298, 370–77, 392–401, 467–505, 551–59, 570–71, 591–99, 601–3, 617–19, 641–46, 765–80, 782–97v, 969, 980–81, 1204–34, 1279v, 1382–63, 1393, 1416–31, 1462.
Justicia. Legajo 199, 405, 817, 984, 999, 1001–2.
Mapas y Planos: Ingenios y Maestres. Legajo 1, 252.
Patronato Real. Legajo 19, 133v–34v, 255, 257.

ARCHIVO HISTÓRICO NATIONAL, MADRID

Ordenes Militares. Expediente 5213.

Published Sources

Adams, William, and Paul Weaver. *Historic Places of St. Augustine and St. Johns County.* St. Augustine: St. Augustine and St. Johns County Chamber of Commerce, 1993.

Agricultural Research Service. *Common Weeds of the United States.* Barre, Mass.: Dover, 1972.

Aguilera, Francisco. *Addendum to Provisional Report.* St. Augustine Restoration Foundation, 1977.

————. *Provisional Report on the Ethnohistory of Social and Economic Stratification and Its Application to the Acquisition of Specified Items of Material Culture and Technology for St. Augustine 1580.* St. Augustine Restoration Foundation, 1977.

American Bible Society. *Good News Bible: The Bible in Today's English Version.* Nashville: Thomas Nelson, 1989.

America's Fascinating Indian Heritage. Pleasantville, N.Y.: Reader's Digest Association, 1978.

Apple, Russell A. *Hawaiian Thatched House: Use—Construction—Adaptation.* San Francisco: National Park Service, 1971.

Aries, Philippe. *Centuries of Childhood.* New York: Knopf, 1962.

Barrientos, Bartolomé. *Pedro Menéndez de Avilés, Founder of Florida.* Translated by Anthony Kerrigan. Gainesville: University of Florida Press, 1965.

Bealer, Alex W. *Old Ways of Working Wood.* Barre, Mass., 1972.

Bennett, Charles E. *Settlement of Florida.* Gainesville: University of Florida Press, 1968.

Blandford, Percy W. *Country Craft Tools.* New York: Funk and Wagnalls, 1976.

Brenan, Gerald. *South From Granada.* Middlesex, U.K.: Penguin, 1963.

Brockman, C. Frank. *Trees of North America.* New York: Golden Press, 1968.

Bushnell, Amy. *The King's Coffer: Proprietors of the Spanish Florida Treasury, 1565–1702.* Gainesville: University Presses of Florida, 1981.

————. *The Menéndez Marqueses and Their Ranch at La Chua.* St. Augustine: Center for Historic Research, 1977.

————. "The Noble and Loyal City, 1565–1668." In *The Oldest City,* edited by Jean Parker Waterbury. St. Augustine: St. Augustine Historical Society, 1983.

Cáceres, Alonso de. *Discurso sobre la población de la costa de la Florida.* Translated by Albert Manucy. In *Catalogue of Unpublished Manuscripts Relating to Florida,* by Woodbury Lowrey, vol. 2. Washington, D.C.: Library of Congress, n.d.

Caro Baroja, Julio. *Los Vascos.* Madrid: Ediciónes Istmo., 1971.

————. *Vasconiana.* Madrid: Ediciónes Minotauro, 1957.

Chaney, Edward. *Report on the 1985 Excavations at the Fountain of Youth Park Site, St. Augustine.* Gainesville: Florida Museum of Natural History, 1987.

Chatelain, Verne E. *The Defenses of Spanish Florida, 1565–1763.* Washington, D.C.: Carnegie Institution of Washington, 1941.

Connor, Jeanette Thurber. "Nine Old Wooden Forts." *Florida Historical Quarterly* 4 (1925): 103–11, 171–80.

————, trans. and ed. *Colonial Records of Spanish Florida*. 2 vols. DeLand: Florida State Historical Society, 1925–30.

Cusick, James G. "Report on the 1993 Excavations at the Nombre de Dios Site (8-SJ-34): The Search for St. Augustine's Early Forts." Unpublished manuscript on file, Florida Museum of Natural History, Gainesville.

Deagan, Kathleen. *Archaeological Strategy in the Investigation of an Unknown Era: Sixteenth Century St. Augustine*. Tallahassee: Florida State University, 1978.

————. "Culture in Transition: Assimilation and Fusion among the Eastern Timucua." In *Tacachale*, edited by J. T. Milanich and S. Proctor. Gainesville: University Presses of Florida, 1978.

————. "Introduction: Summary Interpretation of 1991 Archaeological Field Work at the Fountain of Youth Park Site." In *Report on the 1992 Excavations at the Fountain of Youth Park*, by C. Gardner Gordon. Tallahassee: Florida Department of State, 1992.

————. "The Material Assemblage of Sixteenth-Century Spanish Florida." *Historical Archaeology* 12 (1978): 25–50.

————. "Research and Exhibit Plan for a 1580 Timucua Village near St. Augustine, Florida." Tallahassee: Florida State University, 1979.

————. "Spanish St. Augustine: America's First Melting Pot." *Archaeology* 32 (1980): 22–30.

————. *Spanish St. Augustine: The Archaeology of a Colonial Creole Community*. New York: Academic Press, 1983.

————. "St. Augustine: America's First Urban Enclave." *North American Archaeologist* 3 (1982): 190, 198–99.

Deagan, Kathleen, John Bostwick, and Dale Benton. "A Sub-Surface Survey of the St. Augustine City Environs." Unpublished manuscript on file, Historic St. Augustine Preservation Board.

DeCoste, Fredrik. *First Child of Spanish Florida*. Jacksonville: Convention Press, 1965.

Diderot, Denis. *A Diderot Pictorial Encyclopedia of Trades and Industry*. New York: Dover Publications, 1959.

Dirección General de Arquitectura. *Plan Nacional de Mejoramiento de la Vivienda en los Poblados de Pescadores*. Madrid: Ministerio de la Gobernación, 1942–46.

Dunkle, John R. *Matanzas Inlet: A Geographic Analysis of Sequential Changes*. St. Augustine: Castillo de San Marcos National Monument Library, National Park Service, 1964.

————. *St. Augustine, Florida: A Study in Historical Geography*. Ann Arbor, Mich.: University Microfilms, 1955.

Espiago, Cosmén de. "My Grandmother's House in Asturias." *El Escribano*, no. 51 (1964): 6–9.

Feagin, Jackie. "'Diggers' Hope to Find Menendez Colony Site." *St. Augustine Record*, May 4, 1985.

Feduchi, Luis. *Itinerarios de Arquitectura Popular en España*. Barcelona: Editorial Blume y Editorial Labor, 1974.

Fernández-Sardina, Ricardo. *Preliminary Field Report of Archaeological Investigations at the Ximénez-Fatio Annex*. (SA 34-2b), St. Augustine. Gainesville: Florida State Museum, 1990.

Fletcher, Banister. *A History of Architecture on the Comparative Method*. New York: Charles Scribner's Sons, 1931.

Flores, Carlos. *Arquitectura Popular Española*, vols. 1–5. Madrid: Aguilar, S.A., 1973–77.

Florida Division of Forestry. *Forest Trees of Florida*. Tallahassee: Florida Department of Agriculture and Consumer Services, 1977.

Gannon, Michael V. *The Cross in the Sand: The Early Catholic Church in Florida, 1513–1870*. Gainesville: University of Florida Press, 1965.

Garcia, Genaro. *Dos Antiquas Relaciones de la Florida*. Translated by Albert Manucy. Mexico: Tip. y Lit. de J. Aguila y Vera y Compañia.

García Fernández, Efren, and José Luis. *España Dibujada: I, Asturias and Galicia*. Madrid: Ministerio de la Vivienda, 1972.

Goggin, John M. *Indian and Spanish Selected Writings*. Miami: University of Miami Press, 1964.

Gordon, C. Gardner. *Report on the 1992 Excavations at the Fountain of Youth Park*. Summary Project Report, Division of Historical Resources. Tallahassee: Florida Department of State, 1992.

Hoffman, Paul. "Garrison List, November 19, 1578." Unpublished manuscript, Center for Historic Research, St. Augustine.

———. *Guard Duty, 1566–1595*. St. Augustine: Center for Historic Research, n.d.

———. [Notes on the design of certain sixteenth-century Spanish ordnance]. Unpublished manuscript on file, Center for Historic Research, St. Augustine, 1976.

———. *Photographs of Certain Ordnance Specimens at the Museo del Ejército*. Madrid, 1975.

———. *Revised List of Characters, 1576*. St. Augustine: Center for Historic Research.

———. "Skirmishing Drill with Arcabuz 1592." From Eguiluz 1595 edition. St. Augustine: Center for Historic Research.

———. "St. Augustine 1580: The Research Project." *El Escribano* 14 (1977): 5–19.

———. "A Study of Defense Costs, 1565–1585: A Quantification of Florida History." *Florida Historical Quarterly* 51 (1973): 401–22.

———. *Table of Organization, St. Augustine 1576–1584*. St. Augustine: Center for Historic Research.

Hoffman, Paul, and Eugene Lyon. "Accounts of the Real Hacienda, Florida, 1565–1602." *Florida Historical Quarterly* 48 (1969): 57–69.

———. *Characteristics of the Population in St. Augustine ca. 1580.* St. Augustine: Center for Historic Research, 1976.

———. "Factors' Accounts, 1591–1594." *AGI, Contaduría General, Legajo* 948.

———. *Information on St. Augustine Personnel c. 1580 from Study of the Garrison Musters.* St. Augustine: Center for Historic Research.

———. *Notes from Personal Property Inventories.* St. Augustine: Center for Historic Research, n.d.

———. *Notes on 16th Century Ordnance, from Spanish Archives in Madrid, Sevilla and Simancas.* St. Augustine: Center for Historic Research, 1975.

———. *A Preliminary Report on the Layout of St. Augustine, Florida, ca. 1580.* St. Augustine: Center for Historic Research, n.d.

———. *Reconstruction of a Wooden Fort Similar to the Fourth and Fifth Wooden Forts of St. Augustine, 1571–1585.* St. Augustine: Center for Historic Research, 1973.

Hoffman, Paul, Eugene Lyon, Albert Manucy, and William Rolleston. *Personnel Reservoir.* St. Augustine: Center for Historic Research, 1976.

Hoyos, Nieves. *La Casa Tradicional en España.* Madrid: Publicaciones Españolas, 1959.

Irving, Washington. "A Moorish Palace." In *The Alhambra.* Masterpieces of the World's Best Literature, vol. 5. New York: Classic Printing, 1910.

Jacksonville Florida Tourguide Map. New York: Rand-McNally, 1973.

Kelly, J. F. *Early Domestic Architecture of Connecticut.* New York: Dover Publications, 1963.

Lampérez y Romea, Vicente. *Arquitectura Civil Española de los Siglos I al XVIII,* vol. 1. Madrid: Editorial Saturnino Galleja, 1922.

Levellier, Roberto. *Organización de la Iglesia y Ordenes Religiosas en la Virreinate del Peru en el Siglo XVI,* vol. 2. Madrid: Sucessores de Rivadeneyra, 1919.

Loriga, José Antonio. "Sección de Humor." *Arquitectura* (January 1975).

Lowery, Woodbury. *Catalogue of Unpublished Manuscripts Relating to Florida.* Transcripts from Spanish and French archival documents, vols. 2 and 3. Washington, D.C.: Library of Congress, n.d.

Lucuze, Pedro de. *Principios de Fortificacion.* Barcelona: Tomás Piferrer, 1772.

Lyon, Eugene. "Analysis of the 'Clay Case.'" *AGI, Escribanía de Cámara* 154-A, f. 551v–59, 1576. St. Augustine: Center for Historic Research, n.d.

———. "Analysis of the 'Livestock-Fish-Banquet-Game' Case: vs. Captain Juan de Junco, 1569–1570." *AGI, EC* 154-A, folio 1203v. St. Augustine: Center for Historic Research, n.d.

————. "Cultural Brokers in 16th Century Spanish Florida." Paper presented at Johns Hopkins University, Baltimore, 1987. St. Augustine: Center for Historic Research.

————. *The Enterprise of Florida: Pedro Menéndez and the Spanish Conquest of 1565–1568*. Gainesville: University Presses of Florida, 1976.

————. *Forts Caroline and San Mateo—Vulnerable Outposts*. Fort Caroline National Memorial, Florida, 1982.

————. *Letter to Rolleston and Manucy, 15 August 1978: Report on research in Spanish Archives*. St. Augustine: Center for Historic Research.

————. *Santa Elena: A Brief History*. Institute of Archeology and Anthropology. Columbia: University of South Carolina, 1984.

————. "St. Augustine 1580: The Living Community." *El Escribano* 14 (1977): 20–33.

————. *Towards a Typology of Spanish Colonial Nails*. St. Augustine: Center for Historic Research, 1979.

Manucy, Albert. *Artillery Through the Ages: A Short Illustrated History of Cannon, Emphasizing Types Used in America*. Washington, D.C.: National Park Service, 1943.

————. "Building Materials in 16th Century St. Augustine." *El Escribano* 20 (1983): 51–71.

————. Catalog of Photographs: Spain 1962–1963 series (Notebook C, with index); Spain 1973–1974 series (in album).

————. "Coming of the Corsair." *El Escribano* 26 (1989): 33–58.

————. Fieldbooks I–IX, Spain 1962–1974.

————. *Florida's Menéndez: Captain General of the Ocean Sea*. St. Augustine: St. Augustine Historical Society, 1992.

————. "The Folk Architecture of Spain." In *Old Cities of the New World: Proceedings of the Pan American Symposium on the Preservation and Restoration of Historic Monuments*. St. Augustine, 1967.

————. *The Fort Plan*. Scale drawings. St. Augustine: Center for Historic Research, 1978.

————. *Furnishing Plan for the 1580 Fort at San Agustín*. St. Augustine: Center for Historic Research, 1978.

————. *The History of Castillo de San Marcos and Fort Matanzas from Contemporary Narratives and Letters*. Washington, D.C.: National Park Service, 1943.

————. *The Houses of St. Augustine*. St. Augustine: St. Augustine Historical Society, 1962.

————. Library Notebooks I–V, Spain 1962–1963.

————. "The Man Who Was Pedro Menéndez." *Florida Historical Quarterly* 44 (1965): 67–80.

———. *Marine Exhibits for St. Augustine 1580.* St. Augustine: Center for Historic Research, 1978.

———. Measured Drawings Notebook, no. 1, Galicia and Asturias, Spain 1962–1963.

———. Measured Drawings Notebooks, No. 1, H1–H7, Spain 1962–1963.

———. Museo del Ejército, Exhibits of 15th and 16th Century Ordnance Specimens, Madrid.

———. Museum and Archival Notes, April–May 1962.

———. *Outline of Interpretation for St. Augustine 1580.* St. Augustine: Center for Historic Research, 1979.

———. Personal Interview with Architectural Historian Efren García Fernández, Oviedo, 1974.

———. Personal Interview with Director Rafael Fernández-Huidobro, Escuela Técnica Superior de Arquitectura, Madrid, 1974.

———. Personal Interview with Ignacio Alvarez Castelao, Architect. (Fieldbook I.)

———. Personal Interview with Joaquín de Yrízar, 1962 (Fieldbook I).

———. Photographs: Spanish Folk Architecture 1962–1963, 1973–1974, and 1981. Albums plus slide files.

———. *Plot Plan: The 1580 Town.* St. Augustine: Center for Historic Research, 1979.

———. *Preliminary Study of Artillery at the Fort of St. Augustine in 1580.* St. Augustine: Center for Historic Research, 1975.

———. *Recommendations for Timucua Structures.* St. Augustine: Center for Historic Research, 1981.

———. *Report on Relics from 1923 Excavation of Fortification Site on Parris Island, South Carolina.* St. Augustine: National Park Service, 1957.

———. "Tapia or Tabby." *Journal of the Society of Architectural Historians* 11, no. 4 (1952): 32–33.

———. "Toward Re-Creation of 16th Century St. Augustine." *El Escribano* 14 (1977): 1–4.

———. *The Town Plan for St. Augustine 1580.* St. Augustine: Center for Historic Research, 1977.

———. *Traditional Timberframe in Spain.* St. Augustine: Center for Historic Research, 1974.

———. "Two Pieces of Antique Ordnance." Unpublished manuscript plus measured drawings. St. Augustine: Center for Historic Research, 1981.

Manucy, Albert, and Evalina Manucy. Typical Asturian Houses, sketched from photograph collection of Don Francisco Sarandeses Pérez, 1962.

McDowell, Bart, and Albert Manucy. "The Changing Face of Old Spain." *National Geographic Magazine* (March 1965): 291–339.

Méndez de Canzo, Gonzalo. Papers Relating to the Sale of the Governor's St. Augustine House. *AGI, Santo Domingo* 82 (1603–1604). St. Augustine: Center for Historic Research, 1983.

Mendoza Grajales, Francisco López de. "Relación." In Eugenio Ruidíaz y Caravía, *La Florida: Su Conquista y Colonización por Pedro Menéndez de Avilés*. Madrid: Los Hijos de J. A. García, 1893–1894.

Menéndez de Avilés, Pedro. Lista de la gente de guerra, 1565–1569. *AGI, Contaduría General* 941, 1. St. Augustine: Center for Historic Research.

———. Ordinances. *AGI, Justicia* 999, no. 2, ramo 9 (September 1566).

———. Supplies Furnished by Pedro Menéndez de Avilés for the Florida Expedition, 1565. *AGI, Escribanía de Cámara* 1,024-A.

Menéndez Marquez, Juan. Accounts of Payment to Juan Sánchez, 27 June 1592. *AGI, Contaduría General* 949. St. Augustine: Center for Historic Research.

Menéndez Marquez, Pedro. *Relación de la victoria que el general Pero Menéndez Marques consiguió en el Puerto de Sn. Mateo, 1580. AGI, Simancas, Legajo* 12 of *Papeles diversos*. St. Augustine: Center for Historic Research.

———. "To the Crown, March 25, 1580." In *Colonial Records of Spanish Florida*, 2, translated and edited by Jeanette Thurber Connor, 282. 1925, 1930.

Menéndez Marquez, Pedro, et al. "Investigation Made of Drake's Sacking, Robbing and Burning the Fort and the Royal Chests, 1586." In Lowery, *Catalogue of Unpublished Manuscripts Relating to Florida*, vol. 3.

———. "Investigation of Negligence of the Royal Officials in Custody of the Royal Chest, 1588." In Lowery, *Catalogue of Unpublished Manuscripts Relating to Florida*, vol. 2.

———. "Services of Juan Ramirez de Contreras During the Drake Raid." In Lowery, *Catalogue of Unpublished Manuscripts Relating to Florida*, vol. 3.

Menéndez Pidal, Ramón, and Samuel Gili Gaya. *VOX: Diccionario Ilustrado de la Lengua Español*. Barcelona: Publicaciones y Ediciones Spes, 1953.

Mestas, Hernando de. *Mapa de Pueblo, Fuerte y Cano de San Agustín*. In Verne E. Chatelain, *The Defenses of Spanish Florida 1565 to 1763*. Washington, D.C.: Carnegie Institution of Washington, 1941.

Ministerio de Obras Públicas. *Mapa Oficial de Obras Públicas*. Servicio de Publicaciones, 4th and 10th eds.

Morison, Samuel Eliot. *Admiral of the Ocean Sea, A Life of Christopher Columbus*. Boston: Little, Brown, 1942.

Morla, Tomás de. *Tratado de Artillería*, 3 vols. Madrid: Imprenta Real, 1784.

Morris, William (ed.). *The American Heritage Dictionary of the English Language.* Boston and New York: American Heritage and Houghton Mifflin, 1970.

Morton, H. V. *A Stranger in Spain.* New York: Dodd, Mead, 1955.

Muller, John. *Treatise of Artillery.* London: John Millan, 1757.

Peterson, Charles E. *The French in the Mississippi Valley.* Urbana: University of Illinois Press, 1965.

———. *The Rules of Work of the Carpenters Company.* Philadelphia: Bell Publishing, 1971.

———, ed. *Building Early America.* Radnor, Penn.: Chilton Publishing, 1976.

Rebolledo, José A. *Construcción General.* Madrid, 1876.

Rodríguez Becerra, Salvador. *Etnografía de la Vivienda: El Aljarafe de Sevilla.* Seville: Universidad de Sevilla, 1973.

Rojas, María Teresa de. *Indice y Extractos del Archivo de Protocolos de la Habana: 1578–1585. Protocolo de Juan de Pérez de Barroto, Bernaldo de Valdés and Pero Sánchez v. Luis Hernández, Protocolo de Martín Calvo de la Puerta.* Havana: Imprenta Ucar, Garcia y Campañia, 1950–1957.

Ruidíaz y Caravía, Eugenio. *La Florida: Su Conquista y Colonización por Pedro Menéndez de Avilés,* 2 vols. Madrid: Hijos de J. A. García, 1893–1894.

San Miguel, Andrés de (Albert Manucy, trans.). "Relación de los Trabajos que la Gente de una Nao Padecio." In Genaro García, *Dos Antiguas Relaciones de la Florida.* Mexico: Tip. y Lit. de J. Aguila y Vera y Compañia, 1902.

"Sands of Time," *St. Augustine Record,* 10 June 1935, pp. 8, 10–11.

Shepard, Herschel E. *Reconstruction of 1580 Wooden Fort for St. Augustine Restoration, Inc.* (11 sheets) St. Augustine: Center for Historic Research, 1980.

Smith, James M. *Before the White Man: The Prehistory of St. Johns County, Florida.* St. Augustine: Historic St. Augustine Preservation Board, 1985.

Soil Conservation Service. *Soil Survey of St. Johns County, Florida.* Washington, D.C.: U.S. Department of Agriculture, 1983.

Solís de Meras, Gonzalo (J. T. Connor, trans.). *Pedro Menéndez de Avilés.* Gainesville: University of Florida Press, 1964.

South, Stanley. *Testing Archeological Sampling Methods at Fort San Felipe, 1983.* Columbia: Institute of Archeology and Anthropology, University of South Carolina and the National Science Foundation, 1984.

Spain and Portugal. New York: Baedeker's Touring Guides, 1959.

Spalding, Thomas. "Tabby Wall Construction." *Southern Agriculturalist*

3, part 1 (December 1830). Collections of the Georgia Historical Society, I, 273.

Torres Balbas, Leopoldo. "La Vivienda Popular en España." In *Folklore y Costumbres de España*, vol. 3. Barcelona: Casa Editorial Alberto Martin, 1934.

U.S. Department of Agriculture. *Common Weeds of the United States*. New York: Dover, 1971.

Velázquez de la Cadena, Mariano, et al. *A New Pronouncing Dictionary of the Spanish and English Languages*. Chicago and New York: Wilcox and Follett, 1952.

Vigneras, L. A. "Fortificaciónes de la Florida." *Anuario de Estudios Americanos* 16 (1959): 543.

Vigón, Jorge. *Historia de la Artillería Española*, 3 vols. Madrid: Consejo Superior de Investigaciones Científicas, Instituto Jerónimo Zurita, 1947.

Waterbury, Jean Parker (ed.). *The Oldest City: St. Augustine, Saga of Survival*. St. Augustine: St. Augustine Historical Society, 1983.

Weber, David J. *The Spanish Frontier in North America*. New Haven and London: Yale University Press, 1992.

Webster's New Universal Unabridged Dictionary. New York: Dorset and Baber, 1979.

Wells, H. G. *Outline of History*. Garden City, N.Y.: Garden City Publishing, 1931.

Wilgus, A. Curtis, and Raul D'Eca. *Latin American History*. New York: Barnes and Noble, 1963.

Wilson, Samuel Jr. "Gulf Coast Architecture." In *Spain and Her Rivals on the Gulf Coast*. Pensacola: Historic Pensacola Preservation Board, 1971.

Wolfkill, Lyle A., Wayne A. Dunlap, and Bob M. Gallaway. *Handbook for Building Homes of Earth*. Greeley, Colo.: Rammed Earth Institute International, n.d.

Yrízar, Joaquín de. *Las Casas Vascas*. San Sebastián, Spain: Librería Internacional, 1929.

Yrízar, Joaquin de, and Fausto Arocena. *La Casa de Zumalacarregail*. San Sebastián, Spain: Diputación de Guipúzcoa, 1948.

Zurita Ruiz, José. *Diccionario de Construcción*. Barcelona: Ediciónes CEAC, 1955.

Index

Page numbers in italics refer to illustrations.

loblolly pine (Pinus taeda), 39
locks, 60, 98
lofts, 63
loggias, 63, 91, 115, 119, 122
longleaf pine (Pinus palustris), 55, 94
López, Father, 11
Lorigo, José Antonio, 66
lots, types of, 62, 121, 143, 145
lower class: description of, 61; houses, 76–89
Lucuze, Pedro de, 29
lumber. See wood
Lyon, Eugene, xv, 7, 13

Maldonado, Diego, 30
maps: Boazio, 41, 48; de Mestas, 42; of forts, 30, 33, 34, 43; of inlets, 31; of Timucuan territory, 12, 14
Marrero, Julio, xiii
masonry, 58–59, 100. See also tabby
Matanzas Bay, 30, 33
Matanzas Inlet, 12
Matanzas River, 31
Méndez de Canzo, Gonzalo, Governor, 58, 92, 110
Menéndez de Avilés, Pedro, Governor, 7, 15, 28, 29, 62, 102; background of, 6–7; and colonization of St. Augustine, 7–9, 11; and relationship with Indians, 13
Menéndez Marquez, Pedro, Governor, 32, 113, 118, 121, 122
Merriam, John, Dr., xii, 1
mess groups, 62–63, 88–89
Mestas, Hernando de, Ens., 42
Mexico, 16
middle class: description of, 61; houses, 90–109
Morales, Leonor de (Argüelles), 111, 113
Mordazo, Juan, 84, 86
mortar. See lime; masonry; tabby
mutiny, garrison, 29
myrtle oak (Quercus myrtifolia), 39, 40

nails, 19, 102–3

Newton, Earle, xiii
Nombre de Dios, 4, 11, 43, 49
North Beach (Vilano), 31
Nuestra Señora de los Remedios, 42

officers' quarters, 36, 37
Olmos, Alonso de, 107, 108–9
Orange period, 2
orientation, of houses, 66–67, 67
outbuildings, 16, 58, 63, 78, 115
oval plan structure, 14, 15, 21, 21–22, 23
oyster shells. See shells

pale. See fences
palisades, 14, 33, 34, 56
palmetto. See cabbage palm
Palm Valley, 58
Palos de la Frontera (Spain), 69
Pellicer Series, 59, 83. See also clay
peonía lots, 62, 121, 145
Philip II (Spain), 6–7, 8
Pinus elliottii. See slash pine
Pinus palustris. See longleaf pine
Pinus taeda. See loblolly pine
pit saw, 102
plants, role of native, 19. See also names of individual plants
plot plans, 63, 88; boardinghouses, 88; lower-class houses, 85, 86, 87; middle-class houses, 91, 104, 107; smithies, 106; upper-class houses, 111, 115, 119, 120
Plot Plans: The 1580 Town (Manucy), xv
poles, 22, 56, 71
Pomar, Doña María de (Junco), 110, 118
pond cypress (Taxodium var. nutans), 55
population, of San Agustín el Viejo, 32
post-and-beam splices, 129
postmolds, 69
posts: decorative support, 127, 131; foundation-to-roof, 97; hut, 68; king, 131; queen, 131; support, 126; in timberframe structures, 70, 71, 94. See also palisades; poles